THINGS EVERY PIANO PLAYER SHOULD KNOW

Explore Scales, Chords, Technique, Music Theory, Famous Composers, and So Much More!

KATHY STONE

ISBN: 978-1-962496-21-6

For questions, please reach out to
Support@OakHarborPress.com

FREE BONUS

SCAN ME!

GET OUR NEXT BOOK FOR FREE!
Scan or go to:
OakHarborPress.com/Free

TABLE OF CONTENTS

WELCOME TO THE PIANO

In the United States, it's estimated that 21 million people play the piano, and despite all the new instruments, it's still one of the most popular instruments worldwide. There are over 30,000 pianos made each year, ranging from entry level to the world's most expensive piano, which sold for $3.22 million.

If you haven't taken lessons, you might think learning to play piano is impossible, but it's not. Even with limited musical knowledge, you can learn to play piano. You don't need to know how to read music to start, and you don't need to have a special skill or be a prodigy to do it. Step one is to learn to read sheet music; step two is to understand how a piano works and what you should do with it. Step three is to practice, practice, practice.

Why should you learn to play the piano? It's an amazing beginner's instrument that can create simple music and turn it into a masterpiece. The piano also gives you a chance to play pieces created by the greats, like Beethoven's "Moonlight Sonata" and Mozart's "Rondo Alla Turca."

In this book, you'll learn the basics, starting with musical theory and the parts of a piano. You'll improve your skills through various techniques and even learn about the history of the piano and some famous composers.

The piano is featured in almost every genre of music, from country to rock to classical. Piano is a universal language, and music lovers everywhere can enjoy its harmonious melodies. Because it has so many keys, you might fear the piano at first, but it all boils down to seven simple notes that are in all music.

Playing the piano is not only enjoyable and creative, but it also offers health benefits. Piano playing improves your cognitive functions by increasing your concentration, developing critical thinking, and enhancing memory. Playing the piano can also slow age-related cognitive decline and keep you sharp as you get older. The creativity that you exhibit while playing the piano can even affect other aspects of your life, like work or school.

The piano has also been shown to be an effective part of treating stress and easing anxiety. Making music can boost your self-esteem, which is another step toward better emotional health. Plus, while you're learning the piano and using your fingers and hands, you're improving your fine motor skills.

Since there are so many reasons to learn to play the piano, there's only one question left to ask: Why wait any longer?

4

CHAPTER ONE:
THE PIANO & ITS TOOLS

The first step to learning about the piano is to understand the instrument itself. Once you have a better understanding of the parts of the instrument and how they work together, you'll be able to create beautiful music.

THE ANATOMY OF A PIANO

OUTSIDE OF A PIANO

A piano's appearance is deceiving; beneath the surface lie many vital working parts.

Lid: The piano lid covers the internal parts, and you can lift it when repairs or tuning are needed. Depending on the piano, a lid can also help control the sounds the instrument produces by changing the acoustics.

Lid prop: If a piano can be played with an open lid, there will be a lid prop to hold it open.

Music rack or desk: When you're playing the piano, it's often necessary to have sheet music or a music book open. Sheet music is your guide to how to play the song and make the sounds you want. The music rack holds your music to make reading easier.

Keyboard: The keyboard is the part of the piano that you'll be using the most, so being familiar with it is important. A keyboard is composed of 88 keys, with 52 white keys and 36 black keys. The individual keys represent different notes, and playing them in the right combination allows you to produce the music you want.

Fallboard: The fallboard is the cover that comes down to cover the keys when a piano isn't being played. It's important to have the keys covered so that they don't get broken or overexposed to humidity, heat, and dust.

Cabinet: The rest of the outside protective hull of a piano is called a *cabinet*. The cabinet determines what color, finish, and size your piano is. While most pianos function basically the same inside, the outside can be customized to your liking.

Pedals: There are usually two or three pedals on a piano, and each pedal changes the sound the keys produce.

Legs: The legs support of the piano, stabilizing and evenly distributing its weight. Pianos traditionally have three legs: a bass leg on the left side of the keyboard, a treble leg on the right side of the keyboard, and a point leg on the side farthest from the keyboard.

INSIDE THE PIANO

Inside the piano is where the magic and the music happen. There are many moving parts that work together to create sound. Knowing how the sounds are created can lead to a better appreciation of the piano as an instrument and enable you to play it to its fullest potential.

Soundboard: The soundboard is a critical part of the piano because it allows the piano to produce the unique sounds it's known for. It is often called the "heart" of the piano. The best material for a soundboard is Sitka spruce; the spruce absorbs the higher-pitched sounds to leave a richer sound behind. Ash, cedar, and alder wood are also commonly used.

Strings: Usually made from a blend of high-carbon steel and copper, the strings are what produce the sound by vibrating against the frame when hit by the hammers.

Hammers: The hammers are connected to the keys and hit the strings. They are pieces of wood covered in felt that vibrate until stopped by the backcheck to end the sound.

Damper: The damper is connected to one of the pedals and controls the sound by stopping the vibrations on the strings.

Tuning pin: The tuning pin is used to tighten or loosen the pins that hold the strings. It helps set the sound of the piano.

Key frame: One of the more important parts of the piano, the key frame is what the entire keyboard sits on. If something stops working on your piano, the key frame can be pulled out because it's held in place with rails and pins.

Rim: The piano is enclosed in a wooden frame called a *rim*. It's important for the rim to be strong and reflect sound well, or the music won't be as vibrant.

Lock rail: The wooden board in front of the keyboard that helps hold it in place is called the *lock rail*.

Hitch pin: A hitch pin is a metal pin that the strings are attached to opposite the tuning pin.

Bridges: The wooden board that connects the strings to the soundboard is called a *bridge*. Bridges help amplify the sound.

Agraffe: The small pieces that look like hooks and hold the strings in place are the *agraffe*. They're usually made of brass.

HOW A PIANO IS CONSTRUCTED

It requires many steps to produce a high-quality piano. Someone who specializes in building pianos is called a *piano technician* or *piano builder*. They are extremely talented at their jobs.

The first step to making a piano is to construct the rim. The rim is made of long pieces of wood veneer that are glued together and then laminated to create a flexible but strong piece of wood.

Depending on the maker and brand, a piano can have between 6 and 10 pieces of veneer.

The manufacturer also determines the species of wood. Maple, mahogany, spruce, and beech are commonly used. Having high-quality wood produces a cleaner sound. The use of cheaper material is one reason that less expensive pianos don't have as rich a sound as higher-end or concert-level pianos.

The rim is shaped with heat before the glue completely dries. Once in the correct shape, the glue finishes drying, leaving the rim solid. To complete the rim, a coat of finish is applied. Like any wood, the finish determines what color the piano will be.

With the outside of the piano completed, the interior framework is next. Wooden beams are placed inside to hold the soundboard. These beams are held in place with dovetail joinery, which doesn't require nails or other metal pieces.

The soundboard is made of wood, preferably Sitka spruce or, sometimes, Japanese spruce. The piano's sound hinges on this crucial part. The soundboard is a thin piece of wood that's created by gluing four- to six-inch planks side by side. It's usually no more than half an inch thick; that thickness allows vibrations to travel to the soundboard.

Ribs are placed under the soundboard, allowing the soundboard to rest on the beams while helping the vibrations travel. The ribs, which are also called *belly bars* or *braces*, are placed four to six inches apart. They have tapered ends so that the soundboard isn't too rigid and can vibrate to produce sound.

The strings are then attached. The bass strings are wrapped in copper, while the treble strings are left unwrapped. The different wrapping techniques allow the strings to vibrate at different speeds to create different sounds. One end of the strings is attached to the bridges, and the other end is wrapped around tuning pins.

From there, the piano technician creates the keyboard. Small wooden blocks covered in either black or white plastic make up the 88 keys that are then attached with guide pins. The keys will be attached to the hammers, which will strike the strings.

The hammers are made of light wood like walnut or mahogany. The wood is covered with felt that determines how hard the hammer will hit the string. Softer and harder felt can change the sound of the keys. A piece of leather is then added to the hammer. The felt and leather together are called the *knuckle covering*.

With the addition of the cover and the legs, the piano is complete.

ESSENTIAL PIANO ACCESSORIES

While the piano is obviously the most important piece for making music, some other accessories are needed and will make playing the piano more comfortable.

A piano bench is specially crafted to match the height of the keyboard. A player should be able to sit and have their elbows at almost a 90-degree angle for comfort. The bench should also be wide enough to provide comfortable seating. A cushion can add padding. Most piano benches open to provide storage for sheet music and music books.

While sitting at a piano, your posture is important. Keep you back straight, shoulders back, and head up. If you find yourself leaning down or leaning back to reach the keys, the piano bench isn't the right height and should be adjusted or replaced. Similarly, a pedal extender makes pedals reachable for people who are shorter or for younger players. Pedal extenders are box shaped and sit over the pedals.

To be able to comfortably read a sheet of music, it's a good idea to get a piano lamp for the top of the piano. A piano lamp usually sits on a round base and has a metal shade that's long and narrow, allowing the light to illuminate the sheet music.

When you're not playing, piano covers protect your piano from dust, scratches, direct sunlight, and accidental damage. Covers come in a tarp material or in a padded version for moving. A piano cover can be custom made, but there are also generic piano covers that will work just as well.

Many pianos have casters to make moving the instrument easier. Caster cups, which fit over the legs of a piano, can help protect hardwood floors against scratches, keep the piano from moving, and preserve the piano's sound quality.

Additionally, humidity control systems can help prolong the life of your piano and keep it functional over its lifetime. For optimum sound quality, 40 to 60 percent humidity is best. If your room is too dry or too humid, try adding a humidifier or a dehumidifier.

TUNING & MAINTAINING YOUR PIANO

Keeping your room at the right temperature will reduce how much maintenance your piano needs. Excess humidity can cause wood to warp. Warping can distort the sound and cause the metal pieces to rust over time. If the air is too dry, the wood will contract and crack the soundboard. Keep your piano away from frequently opened doors, windows with direct sunlight, air vents, and fireplaces. These can make regulating the temperature of the room harder.

Because your piano is made of wood, it needs the same basic care as any piece of wood furniture. Dust it at least once a week to prevent dust buildup. Dust can absorb excess moisture and trap it in the veneer. Dust mites rely on moisture in the air to survive, so keeping the humidity down will limit dust and prevent excess moisture from damaging your piano's finish.

Always use wood-approved products or oil when you polish your piano. Test a small area that can't be seen before trying any new product.

Avoid placing drinks on your piano because condensation on a glass can leave rings and damage your finish. It's also not a good idea to place knickknacks and tchotchkes on your piano, as they can dampen sound.

Whenever you aren't playing the piano, make sure that the fallboard is closed over the keyboard. The fallboard is there to keep dust and other loose debris from collecting in the keys and limiting their movement.

Anytime you get ready to play, wash your hands first to avoid grime buildup on the keys. Don't use any harsh chemicals on your keys; instead, use a damp cloth to clean them. If you have an antique piano, there's a chance that the keys are ivory and just need to be wiped down. Talk to a professional about regular maintenance on ivory keys, which need something like guitar wax to protect them.

Bring in someone to tune your piano twice a year when the temperature changes. Tuning means the piano will stay on pitch. Every 5 to 10 years, bring in a professional to check other aspects of your piano. They will make sure all the parts are moving correctly and working like they're supposed to. If at any point you think your piano sounds tinny or off tune, a professional can adjust it.

UNDERSTANDING PIANO PEDALS

There are three types of pedals on a piano: a soft pedal, a sostenuto pedal, and a sustain pedal. Each pedal has a specific job and should be used at different times. Before user-friendly pedals came out, knee levers were more common and an improvement over the hand dampers that were once used. Knee levers are still found on pianos that have been modified to use them instead of pedals, especially for people who have a physical disability in their legs or lower body.

The soft pedal is on the left side. It was patented in 1722 by piano inventor Bartolomeo Cristofori and introduced in the early 18th century. This pedal makes the notes you are playing come out softer and quieter. The soft pedal, also called the *una corda*, works by moving the hammer closer to the string, giving it less room to move when hitting the string. The lack of distance steals some power, producing the softer note with more muted sounds. Having the ability to soften notes gives the composer a chance to tell a story with intimate, reflective, or sad tones.

A famous piece that uses the soft pedal extensively is Chopin's "Nocturnes," a solo produced sometime in the early 1800s. The soft pedal allowed Chopin to create a dreamy sound that has captivated audiences ever since. The piece is about the night, and Chopin used the soft pedal to evoke a serene night. The piece makes it clear that mystery and shadow are part of the night and the song.

The *sostenuto* pedal is in the middle pedal and used to extend sounds. The Boisselot brothers, French piano makers, created the *sostenuto* pedal in 1844. The name translates to "sounds sustained." It wasn't until 1874 that Albert Steinway of Steinway and Sons patented an improved version and began including it on all their pianos.

When the sostenuto pedal is pressed, whatever notes are currently playing will be extended but notes after the pedal has been pressed are not affected. The ability to extend certain notes creates a much more complex and expressive sound.

Maurice Ravel's "Pavane Pour une Infante Défunte" (Pavane for a Dead Princess) is a piece that uses the sostenuto pedal. The piece, written in 1899, is a solo piece about a princess and how she might have danced the pavane, a slow processional dance. The song was commissioned by Princess de Polignac and embraces the *sostenuto* pedal to create a rich harmony.

The middle pedal is not always the sostenuto pedal and is sometimes used for other purposes or can be left off some pianos altogether. The middle pedal might be a bass sustain pedal, extending only bass notes. There is sometimes a practice pedal that makes the piano play quietly so that other people are not disturbed by practice.

The pedal that you will use most commonly is the right pedal, referred to as the *sustain pedal*. Unlike the *sostenuto*, which extends the notes being played only when the pedal is pressed, the sustain pedal will sustain all the notes played the entire time the pedal is pressed down.

When using the sustain pedal, notes blend together to create smooth transitions from one harmony to the next. The sounds will continue to sound even after the keys are released. The pedal works by lifting all dampers off the strings; without the dampers, the string continues to vibrate, and the sounds will resonate.

Another piece by Chopin, part of his "24 Preludes," was not named until it developed the nickname "Raindrop Prelude." Chopin wrote the piece so that the sustain pedal runs the notes together, creating the effect of soft rainfall that transitions into a dark, stormy rain. The pedal helps the raindrops sound connected versus being random notes.

As you gain more experience, you'll learn different ways to use the pedals. There is delayed, or *legato*, pedaling that involves pushing the pedal after a note and then after the next note to create crisp sounds.

Meanwhile, half pedaling involves pushing the pedal down partway instead of all the way down. It allows a pianist to create richer sounds without the sound getting muddy or blurred. There are also some other rarely used techniques that you can learn as you get more advanced, like simultaneous pedaling, preliminary pedaling, and overlap pedaling.

DIFFERENT TYPES
OF PIANOS

GRAND PIANOS

Grand pianos are iconic for their curves and elegant, wing-like shape. They have two straight sides and a curved third side. Grand pianos are recognized for having a lid that props open when being played. They're considered superior pianos because they project more sound and have deeper resonance.

Concert grand piano: Known as the largest piano, the concert grand is used by orchestras to carry sound throughout large venues. The sound of this piano is louder because of its longer strings. Concert grands cost between $100,000 and $200,000 and are rarely found in private homes.

Semi-concert grand piano: Ranging in size from 7 to 8.5 feet, semi-concert grands are used in smaller areas like music halls and recording studios. To invest in a semi-concert grand piano, plan to spend between $50,000 and $150,000.

Parlor grand piano: Ranging in size from 6 to 7 feet, parlor grands work well in large rooms. A parlor grand piano runs from $35,000 to $100,000.

Studio grand piano: Commonly seen in music classrooms and colleges, the studio grand piano is 4 feet, 8 inches wide.

These pianos are built to withstand use by many students for years. A studio grand costs between $25,000 and $80,000, depending on the manufacturer and style.

Baby grand piano: A smaller version of the grand piano, the baby grand ranges from 5 to 5.5 feet and is commonly found in homes. Baby grands are popular because of their small size and rich sound. Plus, they are more affordable, ranging in price from $8,000 to $40,000.

Petite grand piano: The very smallest grand piano, a petite measures under 5 feet. The smallest petite grand can cost $5,000 to $20,000.

UPRIGHT PIANO

While grand pianos produce a richer sound, they take up a lot of space, which isn't practical in most homes. The upright piano is much more compact, and although the sound it produces is somewhat muted, it still can create beautiful music. Upright pianos have vertical strings instead of horizontal.

Full upright: The biggest vertical piano is over 48 inches tall and has the best sound of the upright pianos because of its size. A full upright has a sound that rivals many grands. They are most common in larger homes and small music classes. An upright costs much less than a grand, starting at around $8,000.

Studio upright: Small in size and with shorter strings, a studio upright measures between 44 inches and 48 inches. It's perfect for the homes of casual players or beginners. If you're looking for a studio upright, plan to spend around $6,000 to $12,000, depending on the style, maker, and extra features.

Console piano: A console piano is between 40 inches and 44 inches and is perfect for use at home. It has good volume and range without being as expensive as some of the larger pianos. A console piano doesn't take up as much room and runs from $4,000 to $10,000.

Spinet piano: The smallest of the upright pianos, a spinet measures less than 40 inches. The back of the piano is right above the keyboard, and the strings have limited movement. This causes a less satisfying sound than other pianos but is still wonderful for limited spaces. Spinet pianos start at $1,500, making them some of the most affordable pianos.

ELECTRIC KEYBOARDS

The other option beside the acoustic grand and upright pianos is the electric keyboard. These are convenient because of their smaller size and portability. A keyboard's sound is created digitally, so there aren't any moving parts that need housing. Most electric keyboards only have 61 keys, which means they don't have the range of a traditional piano. However, some higher-end electric pianos have a full-range keyboard.

Electric keyboards are much cheaper than a piano, and many beginners prefer to start with one. You can also regulate the volume for practice. Keyboards don't need the maintenance that acoustic pianos do because there are no moving parts to service.

DIGITAL PIANOS

If you aren't sure if an electric keyboard or acoustic piano is best suited for your needs, there's another option that combines the two. Digital pianos offer a full keyboard of 88 keys and the more traditional sound of an upright or grand.

A digital piano has the advantage of being hardier because there isn't a soundboard that can be affected by temperature and humidity. There are also ways to connect headphones to your digital piano, making it easier to play silently. There are several kinds of digital pianos.

> **Upright digital piano:** This model of digital piano sits against a wall and mimics the appearance of an acoustic piano, which looks nicer in a home. An upright digital piano costs between $1,500 and $6,000.

> **Stage digital piano:** If a piano needs to be moved regularly, a stage digital piano works well. They are called *stage pianos* because they're what bands use when touring. They also look like a more traditional piano. Stage pianos don't have speakers, so you'll need an outside sound system. Ranging from $1,000 to $5,000, stage pianos can be an affordable option for musicians on the move.

> **Grand digital piano:** A grand digital piano looks like a traditional grand piano but doesn't need maintenance. While it might not have the same depth of sound that an acoustic grand does, the digital version provides adjustable volume. Priced from $3,000 to $20,000, a grand digital piano is more budget friendly than the acoustic version.

If you're in the market for a new piano, try checking locally. Many people invest in pianos and realize later on that they don't have the room or that they have less use for the piano than they thought. A used piano will cost less; just make sure to have maintenance done when you get it.

CHAPTER TWO: BUILDING YOUR FOUNDATION

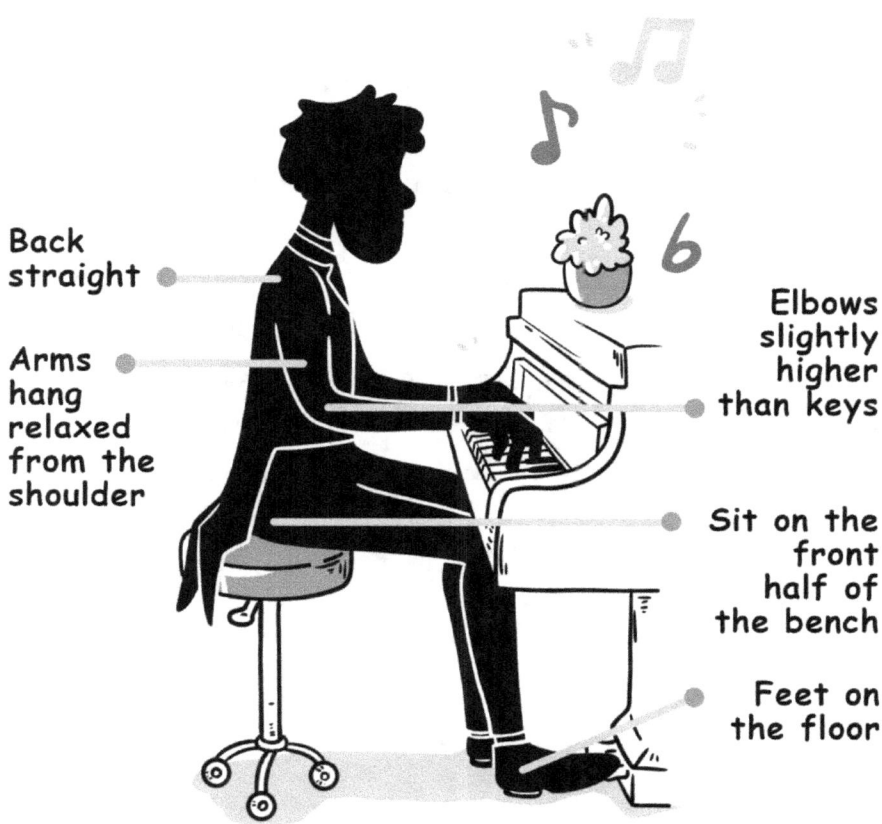

Back straight

Arms hang relaxed from the shoulder

Elbows slightly higher than keys

Sit on the front half of the bench

Feet on the floor

When you're first learning how to play the piano, it can seem overwhelming, but once you break it down, you'll see that the piano isn't hard to master. You'll be creating music to enjoy in no time. Once you become skilled, playing for your family and friends will give you the chance to share your new ability, and everyone loves beautiful music.

BASIC MUSIC THEORY
FOR PIANO PLAYERS

Music theory is the study of the fundamental parts of music and how it's recorded and represented in written form. It introduces the basic building blocks of knowledge that anyone needs to build and expand their musical understanding. Once you know how music works, it becomes easier to read music and play any instrument.

NOTES NAMES

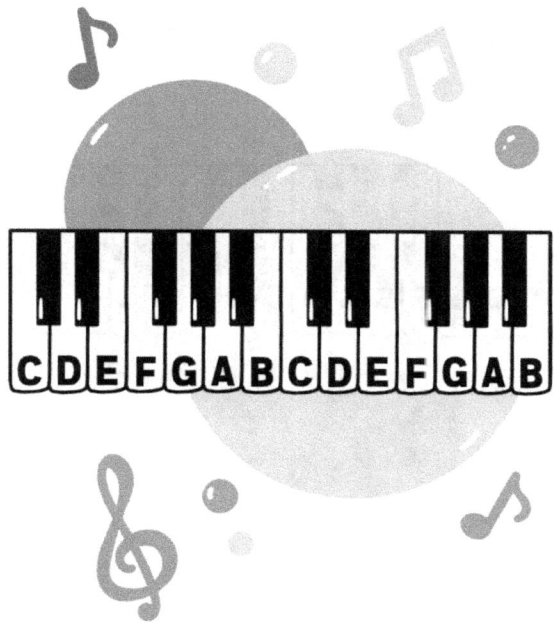

There are seven natural musical notes, each represented by a letter. The letters are C, D, E, F, G, A, and B. The lowest pitch is associated with A and moves up in repeating increments. One of the most commonly used keys on the piano is the middle C because it's the key that's directly in the middle of the keyboard and affects hand placement.

Along with the natural notes, there are sharp and flat versions of each note. These are called *accidentals*, and they change how a note sounds. Depending on the symbols around a note, it might be natural, sharp, or flat.

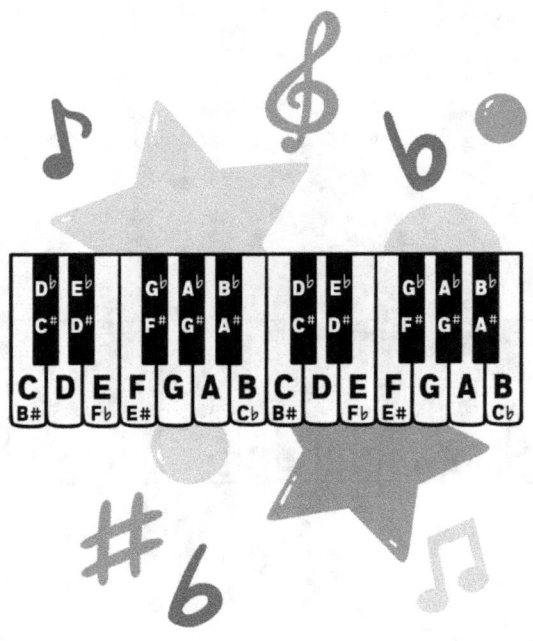

♭ **Flat:** lowers the pitch of a note by a half step

Sharp: raises the pitch of a note by a half step

♮ **Natural:** doesn't change the tone of the note

× **Double sharp:** raises the pitch of a note by a whole step

♭♭ **Double flat:** lowers the pitch of a note by a whole step

Across the keyboard, you have C, C#, D♭, D, D#, E♭, E, F, F#, G♭, G, G#, A♭, A, A#, B♭, B, C, C#, D♭. The keys on your keyboard represent the different versions of each note. Each version of a note has a different sound and is what makes music so expressive.

YOUR KEYBOARD

With 88 keys total, 52 white keys and 36 black keys, each key has a different sound. It's important to understand what each key sounds like. The white keys are at the front, and the black keys sit higher and farther back.

The white keys represent the notes, while the black keys represent certain sharps and flats. On the keyboard, the black keys are grouped in twos and threes. The white keys run continuously.

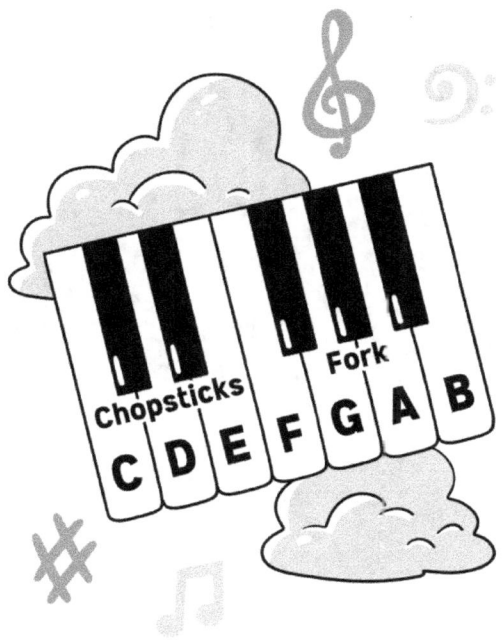

The black keys work well for finding your finger placement. The C key is to the left of the "chopsticks," and the F key is to the left of the "fork." This is true across the board and allows you to know where C and F are at all times.

The keys are broken down into repeating sets called *octaves*. A full piano has seven octaves because the keys repeat seven times. Each octave has five black keys and seven white keys.

After each G key, the next octave starts with an A.

To learn more about the keyboard and the different keys, check out this video.

POSTURE

We talked about a piano bench earlier and how important it is. But before we move on to learning how to read and understand music, you should know the correct way to sit at a keyboard. Posture refers to how you sit in front of your piano and how you place your hands and arms. If you're planning to spend a lot of time in front of your piano, it's important to know how to sit to avoid a sore back or hand cramps.

If you're playing a traditional piano, you will be sitting. Some electric pianos adjust for playing while standing, but for the majority of piano players, sitting is the best option. Whatever kind of chair or bench you use, make sure it's comfortable. If the seat is too hard, add a cushion. The height of your chair or bench is very important and should allow your feet to rest flat on the floor and your arms to be held at a 90-degree angle running parallel to the floor.

If you have to lean over or slouch down to your keyboard, you're sitting too high. If you must reach up, you're too low. While benches are the preferred seating option for most piano players, a chair comes with the benefit of having an adjustable height. If you're struggling to find a seat that allows you to play comfortably, consider using an adjustable chair.

If you've ever seen a concert pianist play, you'll notice they seem to have an almost rigid posture. That isn't because they're worried about how they look on stage; it's because they're worried about getting a sore back.

On the other hand, if you've ever seen a pianist who is playing a wide-ranging piece, moving their hands up and down the keyboard, you'll notice they seem to move with the music. The type of musical piece you are playing can influence your posture as well. As long as you can relax your arms and shoulders, your back position will adjust. Try to keep a straight back, but don't be alarmed if you need to move around a lot to reach keys.

Your hands are essential to playing the piano, and good hand maintenance goes a long way. Trimming your nails is a good start. If you have longer nails and they're hitting against the keys, it can distract from the music. No one wants a beautiful symphony interrupted by *click, click, click.*

HOW TO READ SHEET MUSIC

THE STAFF

To play the piano, you have to understand how to read the notes on sheet music. One of the most recognizable parts of sheet music is the staff. Made up of five lines with four spaces between them, the staff is like the lines on notebook paper. It gives organization to the writing that is music because, just like words, music tells a story too.

Each line and space correspond to a musical note represented by the letters A through G. Those letters tell musicians what they'll be playing. Without the staff to hold the letters, you wouldn't be able to understand what they mean. The letters move alphabetically from A to G in repeating order. The spaces represent F, A, C, and E, while the lines represent E, G, B, D, and F.

It is important to remember the letters, and an easy way to do that is with the mnemonic "Every Good Boy Does Fine." The letters in the spaces are easy because they spell FACE. The letters represent the white keys on a keyboard.

Not all notes fit on the staff. Ledger lines are short horizontal lines that extend past the five lines of the staff to represent the notes that are above and below. Because the piano and other music have so much more range than just the five lines, the ledger lines allow those notes to be shown.

Once you start understanding the different parts of music, it's time to understand how music is recorded on paper.

CLEF

There is a clef at the beginning of every staff. The two main clefs are treble and bass. Normally, the treble is played by the right hand, and the bass clef is played by the left hand.

The treble clef is the most common and looks like a backward fancy S. The bass clef looks like half a heart followed by a colon.

The clef sits at the beginning of the staff.

When you're looking at the staff, the line that runs through the circle of the treble clef is the G note. This G is the G key that's closest to the center of the keyboard. Ascending notes move up the keyboard, and descending notes move down the keyboard.

Another important note is the middle C, which appears on the imaginary line below the treble clef.

Because the two staffs represent different keys on your keyboard, they are both needed. To join both the treble clef and the bass clef, you use a brace and make them one happy family called a *grand staff*.

Once you have a grand staff, it's important to separate it into understandable and easy-to-read parts. To do that, vertical lines called *bar lines* are used to separate the staff into measures. These lines work like a period or comma in a sentence. There are different bar lines, and each has a different meaning:

> **Single:** A single thin line that tells you to move on to the next measure.
>
> **Double:** Two thin lines mark the end of each section.
>
> **Repeat:** When you see a thin line, a thick line, and a colon in a row, it means that you need to go back and repeat that portion of the song.
>
> **End:** One thin line and one thick line let you know when to stop playing at the end of a piece.

MUSICAL NOTES

Notes are to music like the alphabet is to language. They are the building blocks of music. Once you understand how to read notes, you'll be on the way to reading music. To play the piano, you need to read music.

Each note represents several beats, and playing the sounds in the correct order produces music. A note's location on the staff determines what it stands for, but the symbol determines how long you play it. There are lots of notes, but the most common ones are what you need to play most pieces. Starting with the largest note, think of them in terms of percentages.

> **Whole note:** This is the longest note in music. A whole note lasts four beats, making it a longer sound. The whole note looks like a hollow oval. It is 100 percent of four beats.

> **Half note:** Where a whole note is four beats, a half note is only two. The half note looks like a hollow circle with a line sticking up or down. It is 50 percent of four beats.

> **Quarter note:** Like the name suggests, the quarter note represents a quarter of the whole note, or one beat. The quarter note is a solid circle with a line sticking straight up or down. It doesn't matter which way the note is facing because the line placement is just for ease of reading. It is 25 percent of four beats.

Eighth note: An eighth note is one eighth of a whole note. It looks like a quarter note with an added tail. It is 12.5 percent of four beats.

Sixteenth note: The sixteenth note is one quarter of a beat. It looks like it has two flags coming off it. It is 6.25 percent of four beats.

The idea of writing down music has been around as long as civilization. The first written musical recordings were found around 1400 BCE in ancient Babylonia, which is in modern-day Iraq. In 1025, a monk named Guido of Arezzo started arranging music and formed the foundation for how we record music today. He introduced the staff and clef, which allowed music to be arranged in a much more organized manner than before.

Notes, as we recognize them, were not incorporated until the 13th century. It has taken years of trial and error to establish the musical language we have today. Having a universal musical language allows artists to share music, and it connects people across many languages.

The ability to record music also allows us to pass down music to future generations. Before notes and music could be written down, oral history was the only option.

RESTS

Just as notes show when to play, rests indicate when to pause in music. Even though you aren't playing music, you still need to keep count so that you know when to play again.

Rests come in counts, much like notes:

Whole rest: This is the longest rest. It lasts four beats and looks like an upside-down hat.

Half rest: A half rest is two beats long. It looks like a hat sitting right-side up.

Quarter rest: A quarter rest should be held for one beat. It looks like a fancy lightning bolt.

Eighth rest: An eighth rest should be held for half a beat. It looks like a skinny flag on a slanted line.

Sixteenth rest: This is a shorter rest lasting only a quarter of a beat. It looks like two skinny flags coming off a slanted line.

While it might seem like rests aren't an important part of music, they're actually just as important as the notes. Without a rest, you wouldn't be able to create rhythms or make music with dramatic pauses. The rests bring music to life, allowing it to breathe between notes. Any good pianist knows that sometimes you need a rest to create a truly memorable piece of music.

SCALES

In music, a scale is a repeating set of notes played in a specific order that follows the pattern of the intervals. If notes are like letters to make musical words, then scales are like sentences that work together to create a story.

Scales are commonly used by singers to warm up their voices. One of the most famous examples of a scale is from the classic movie *The Sound of Music.* When Maria and the children sing "Do-Re-Mi," they are actually practicing scales.

Most scales are made of eight notes. The notes are very close together because a scale moves up or down the keyboard but doesn't tend to take huge jumps. The scales you will most often hear about are the major scale, the natural minor scale, the harmonic minor scale, and the melodic minor scale.

MAJOR SCALES

The major scale runs in this order: whole step, whole step, half step, whole step, whole step, whole step, and half step. When you apply the letters of the sounds to the formula, you will have something like this:

C major scale: C, D, E, F, G, A, B, C

G major scale: G, A, B, C, D, E, F#, G

D major scale: D, E, F#, G, A, B, C#, D

A major scale: A, B, C#, D, E, F#, G#, A

F major scale: F, G, A, B♭, C, D, E, F

NATURAL MINOR SCALE

The minor scale, also called the *natural minor scale*, has nothing to do with being smaller, but it does sound different. The minor scale follows this pattern: whole step, half step, whole step, whole step, half step, whole step, whole step. Here are the main natural minor scales:

C minor scale: C, D, Eb, F, G, Ab, Bb, C

G minor scale: G, A, Bb, C, D, Eb, F, G,

D minor scale: D, E, F, G, A, Bb, C, D

A minor scale: A, B, C, D, E, F, G, A

E minor scale: E, F#, G, A, B, C, D, E

One of the easiest ways to compose music is by using the scales and then removing or adding notes as you need to create the sounds you're looking for. The scales are just a starting point.

HARMONIC SCALE

The harmonic scale is a small change from the minor scale, but the small change makes a huge difference. The change in sound can create a completely different set of music. A minor scale runs like this: whole step, half step, whole step, whole step, half step, whole step, whole step.

Compare the A minor scale and the A harmonic minor scale:

A minor scale: A, B, C, D, E, F, G, A

A harmonic minor scale: A, B, D, E, F, G#, A

Here are all the main harmonic minor scales:

C harmonic minor scale: C, D, E♭, F, G, A♭, B, C

D# harmonic minor scale: D#, E#, F#, G#, A#, B, C#, D#

A harmonic minor scale: A, B, C, D, E, F, G#, A

E harmonic minor scale: E, F#, G, A, B, C, D#, E

THE MELODIC MINOR

Another scale is the melodic minor scale, also called the *jazz minor*. This minor is often used in jazz music. It goes whole step, half step, whole step, whole step, whole step, whole step, half step.

Compare the A minor scale and the A melodic minor scale:

A minor scale: A, B, C, D, E, F, G, A

A melodic minor scale: A, B, C, D, E, F#, G#, A

Here are all the main melodic minor scales:

C melodic minor scale: C, D, E♭, F, G, A, B, C

G melodic minor scale: G, A, B♭, C, D, E, F#, G

D melodic minor scale: D, E, F, G, A, B, C#, D

A melodic minor scale: A, B, C, D, E, F#, G#, A

E melodic minor scale: E, F#, G, A, B, C#, D#, E

Those of all the minor scales of each kind but there are a few more. The scales run A, A#/B♭, B, C, C#/D♭, D, D#/E♭, E, F, F#/G♭, G, G#/A♭.

INTERVALS

The distances between notes are called the *intervals*. They're like the distance between two points on a map. Just like scales, intervals come in major and minor with an additional perfect. The major intervals sound happier, and minor intervals sound a lot sadder.

The smallest interval on a piano keyboard is a half-step, which could be between the white key D and its sharp. Going from white key to white key is considered a whole step.

> **Half step:** This is the smallest distance on a keyboard. It doesn't matter what color the keys are. A half step goes from C to C# or from E to F since there's no black key.

> **Whole step:** Made of two half steps, a whole skip is like stepping from one key to get to the next one. An example is going from C to D, skipping the black key, or from F to G, skipping the black key.

The distance between the keys is measured by the number of notes that it includes. C to G is a fifth (because it contains C, D, E, F, and G). C to E is a third interval (because it contains C, D, and E). Smaller intervals make the notes sound more connected, while the larger intervals make the notes sound more broken up.

Here are all the intervals:

41

Unison: The distance between two notes that are the same (e.g., C to C)

Second: The distance between two notes that are connected (e.g., C to D or C to D♭)

Third: The distance across three notes (e.g., C to E)

Fourth: The distance across four notes (e.g., C to F)

Fifth: The distance across five notes (e.g., C to G)

Sixth: The distance across six notes (e.g., C to A)

Seventh: The distance across seven notes (e.g., C to B)

Octave: The distance between two notes that are the same on different scales

An octave and a unison can seem a lot alike because they both contain the same note, but a unison is the exact same pitch, while an octave has a full set of eight keys between the two notes.

The "perfect intervals" are unison, fourth, fifth, and octave. The term *perfect* refers to the pure sounds that are made when all the notes are in tune. The rest are considered imperfect.

Once you can recognize the notes and understand how they appear on a staff, it's time to move on to understanding the other parts of music.

TIME SIGNATURE

The time signature tells you the timing of a piece of music. The speed or timing of your song is called the *tempo*. When you are looking at sheet music, there are two numbers on top of each other right behind the clef. That is your time signature. The top number will let you know how many beats are in each measure, and the bottom number will indicate which note gets a full beat.

There are several common time signatures that are used for piano pieces.

> **4/4**: The four on top means that there are four beats in each measure, and the bottom number means that the quarter note is equal to one beat.

> **3/4:** The three means there are three beats in a measure, and the four on the bottom means that the quarter note gets one beat. This is the time signature commonly used in a waltz.

> **2/4:** This gives each measure two beats and keeps the quarter note as one beat.

> **6/8:** With this time signature, each measure will have six beats per measure and the eighth note gets one beat. It is mostly counted in two groups of three beats each.

While you are playing sheet music, these numbers will allow you to find the correct rhythm as the composer intended.

HOW TO USE A METRONOME

A metronome is a tool that keeps steady time with clicks or another receptive sound so that you can learn to play at a consistent pace. Patented in 1815 by Johann Maelzel, the metronome was made popular by Ludwig van Beethoven much later when he included timing marks in his musical scores.

When playing with a metronome, you can set your tempo and stay in time with the intended speed of the musical piece. It measures the beat in a steady way and with a set count. It helps you by letting you keep the correct count as you play the piano. Rhythm is a large part of beautiful music, and the metronome is the tool that helps you keep the time signature.

Set your metronome to the time signature, and you'll be able to hear if you are playing the right beat. It's a great tool for beginners but will continue to be a valuable tool as you gain more experience. Even the most experienced pianist uses metronomes when dealing with difficult counts.

GRACE NOTES

A grace note is a small, miniature note that can be played before a regular note. It's small to indicate it should be played very quickly. They can add style and make a more ornamental sound.

A grace note doesn't count as a beat in the measure because it's played so fast. It adds extra flair to a note giving the note more grace.

LEARNING YOUR FIRST CHORDS

A chord is when you play three or more notes simultaneously using one of both hands. Chords are where music gains harmony. Just like other parts of music, there are several types of chords: major chords, minor chords, diminished chords, augmented chords, and some others. The lowest note in a chord is called the *root note* and is how the chord is named.

The most common way to form a chord is with a triad. A triad is a group of three notes added together. It has the root note, a third, and a fifth. Stacking intervals, like thirds, with a root note creates the chords that allow music to have a mood.

MAJOR CHORD

A major chord comprises a root, a major third, and a perfect fifth.

A C major triad includes C, E, and G.

- Root: C
- Major third: E
- Perfect fifth: G

An E major triad includes E, G#, and B.

- Root: E
- Major third: G#
- Perfect fifth: B

An F major triad includes F, A, and C.

- Root: F
- Major third: A
- Perfect fifth: C

A chord is a major as long as it follows the rule of root, a major third (four half steps above the root), and a perfect fifth (seven half steps from the root).

MINOR CHORD

A C minor triad includes C, E♭, and G.

- Root: C
- Minor third: E♭
- Perfect fifth: G

An E minor triad includes E, G, and B.

- Root: E
- Minor third: G
- Perfect fifth: B

An F minor triad is F, A♭, and C.

- Root: F
- Minor third: A♭
- Perfect fifth: C

A minor chord or triad has a root, a minor third, and a perfect fifth. A minor third is three half steps away from the root, and a perfect fifth remains the same.

CHAPTER THREE: DEVELOPING YOUR TECHNIQUE

Once you grasp the foundational concepts of music, it's time to start looking at some of the more intricate parts.

MELODY, HARMONY, & RHYTHM

Three fundamental terms you'll hear in music are *harmony*, *melody*, and *rhythm*. Understanding these will lead to a deeper comprehension of music.

The melody is the tune from a piece of music. When notes are played one after the other, you are creating a melody. In music, melodies are the main tunes and are supported by harmony. Harmony happens as multiple notes are played together. When music goes from single notes to the richer sound that piano is known for, it's because the pianist is using harmony.

Rhythm refers to the beats in music and how they're spread out during a time sequence. When you clap along with a song, that is often the rhythm. Rhythm is also affected by the length of notes and rests.

MASTERING *ARPEGGIOS*

Arpeggios can be played up or down the keyboard. Most people refer to them as *broken chords* because there aren't three notes being played together but one single note being played one after the other.

Think about it this way: When you play a C major chord, you would play C, E, and G at the same time, but if you're playing an *arpeggio*, then you would play C alone, then E alone, and then G alone in a quick sequence. The notes will sound like they're flowing together.

Arpeggios are used for several things because they're a common part of piano music. Mastering *arpeggios* will improve your technique and dexterity on the keyboard. When you're learning to play *arpeggios*, start slowly because speed needs to be something that you build up. You need to be able to complete *arpeggios* with both hands.

The left-handed *arpeggio* is one of the easiest parts to learn because they follow the same pattern played over and over. While you master more complex chords for your right hand, the left hand can complete a simple arpeggio.

ARTICULATIONS

Musical articulations help you understand how a piece of music is to be played. They add expression to the music and give you more flexibility.

Each articulation produces distinct sounds that are sometimes smooth, short, or accented. The different expressions create more emotion in music. Just like articulation refers to speaking clearly, musical articulation allows your music to deliver the intended emotions or ideas. There are several types of articulations.

LEGATO & STACCATO

Legato is Italian for "smooth." When you are playing notes *legato*, play them smoothly by connecting them together. Avoid breaks in between the notes. Hold your note until the next note is playing so that the notes run together.

Unlike *legato*, *staccato* means to play short, detached notes. Play each note briefly and leave a small gap before playing the next note.

SLURS & TIES

A musical slur is used when notes should be played together smoothly. You'll see this written as a curved line over several notes, indicating that there shouldn't be breaks in between the notes. Slurs should be played *legato*. A slur might cover two notes or as many notes as it needs. They connect different pitches, and you need to focus on smoothness as you are playing those notes.

Ties are different from slurs. A musical tie is a curved line that connects two notes, but unlike the slurs, they are the same pitch. These notes should be played in a continuous sound. Ties might connect two half notes. Instead of playing a half note and then another half note, you would hold the note for the duration of two notes.

While both are curved lines that connect notes, they indicate very different things when you're playing the music. Understanding the difference will allow you to play music how it was intended.

CHOPPY & DETACHED NOTES

Staccato is when you need to play your notes quickly and abruptly. It is represented by a dot over your notes. This is the opposite of how you play when you are playing slurs.

Staccatissimo is a more extreme *staccato* that tells you to play your notes very choppy. *Staccatissimo* looks like a keyhole over the notes.

Portato is another way to play. They are dots like *staccatos* but with a slur over them. This is an in-between form of playing. Play the notes more smoothly than the *staccatos*, but don't run them together like a slur.

ACCENTS

Accents are when you see a symbol that looks like a greater than symbol (>). It means that the note needs to be played louder than the surrounding ones. Put extreme emphasis on that note.

Sforzando is shown as the letters *sfz* over a note. It's very similar to an accent, and the notes need to be played louder. *Sforzando* is an Italian word that means "to give a sudden strong accent," so give it more prominence than accents.

Marcato needs even more pizzazz than the accent and *sforzando*. The symbol for *marcato* looks like an upright triangle with no bottom.

Tenuto looks like a line over notes and needs to be played longer than the other accents. Think of it as the long, strong accent. Several *tenutos* in a row or several *tenutos* with a slur mean that the notes need to be detached and not smoothly together. It's called *tenuto vari*.

Lastly, *fortepiano* tells you to play the note loudly, but the next note needs to be quiet. *Fortepiano* is represented by the letters *fp* over notes.

FERMATA

Fermata is an accent symbol that is used with notes or rests. It tells you to hold that note or rest longer than you would normally. It looks like an arc or semicircle with a dot in it. You can hold that note for longer than usual with no set length.

When playing individually, the player decides how long to hold it, but in an orchestra, the conductor will decide how long to hold it. The fermata is a musical freeze button. It does a good job of adding extra drama to music.

TEMPO MARKINGS

Tempo markings tell you how slow or fast you should play a piece of music. There are many tempos that range from under 24 beats per minute, the slowest, to over 200 beats per minute at the fastest.

Beats per minute (bpm) tells you how many beats should happen in a minute of music. It gives you speed to play. Tempos are shown atop the first bar. Here are some common tempos:

Larghissimo: This is an extremely slow tempo, the slowest, with a pace of 24 bpm or less. Playing this slowly can create a sense of eternity.

Adagissimo **or** *grave*: Very slow and solemn, these tempos fall between 24 and 40 bpm. This speed can come across as heavy or sad. It's often used for serious pieces.

Largo: Slow and broad, between 40 and 66 bpm, this speed creates sense of calm or majesty.

Larghetto: Somewhat slow and broad, *larghetto* is played between 44 and 66 bpm. This speed is peaceful, gentle and might create a tender feeling.

Adagio: This is a slow pace, played with deep expression, ranging from 44 to 66 bpm. It's used to create deep feelings that lean toward contemplation.

Adagietto: A bit faster than *adagio* or slower than *andante*, with a tempo between 46 and 80 bpm; this speed can be used to evoke a delicate or subtle emotion like nostalgia.

Lento: Slow, with a tempo falling between 52 and 108 bpm; this tempo creates a tranquil feeling.

Andante: This is a moderate tempo, like a walking pace, between 56 and 108 bpm. It gives a sense of contentment or light optimism.

Andantino: A tempo slightly faster than andante but slower than moderato; this tempo falls between 80 and 108 bpm. It gives a sense of moving forward, but not quickly, more like an afternoon stroll.

Marcia moderato: This tempo is moderate with a march-like style that falls between 66 and 80 bpm. It can create a sense of order.

Andante moderato: This tempo sits between *andante* and *moderato* at around 80 to 108 bpm. It can sound balanced.

Moderato: This is a medium tempo that falls between 108 and 120 bpm. It creates a feeling of comfort and confidence.

Allegretto: This tempo is moderately fast at a speed between 112 and 120 bpm. The listener will pick up a light and cheerful sound.

Allegro moderato: A tempo close to *allegro* but slightly slower between 116 and 120 bpm; this speed gives off a positive, happy energy.

Allegro: Fast and lively with a range of 120 to 156 bpm, this speed conveys excitement and joy.

Molto allegro or *allegro vivace*: Faster and livelier than *allegro* at 124 to 156 bpm, this speed is a step up in the excitement and energy level.

Vivace: Lively and quick with a tempo between 156 and 176 bpm, it creates a stronger feeling of excitement.

Vivacissimo and *allegrissimo*: This speed is very fast and bright, between 172 and 176 bpm. Moving from joyful to exuberant, these tempos can create an even more extreme feeling.

Presto: This tempo is very fast at a speed of 168 to 200 bpm. At this speed, the listeners might feel breathless and consider the music thrilling or dramatic.

Prestissimo: This is the fastest tempo, exceeding 200 bpm. It can be challenging to play this fast, but it can express frenzy or overwhelming exhilaration.

THE ROLE OF DYNAMICS IN PIANO PLAYING

Dynamics refers to how loudly or softly you play a piece of music. The dynamics that the piece is written with will depend on the mood the composer is trying to create. To determine how loudly or quietly you need to play, there are symbols in between the treble clef and the bass clef.

PIANISSISSIMO (ppp)

At this level, the music is barely whispered to the audience and seems hardly real. The "barely there" playing can create a feeling of fragility or delicacy for the audience, conveying the idea that the music could disappear at any moment. Because of the fleeting feeling of the music, the audience has to listen closely, and it can be a good way to draw a listener in.

For an example, listen to Claude Debussy's Clair de Lune, where he uses pianississimo to signal an ethereal, otherworldly atmosphere. The soft sounds really demonstrate how music can float and have a dream-like mood.

PIANISSIMO (pp)

Played just a bit louder than *pianississimo,* this volume is often used to create a sense of intimacy or mystery. The gentle sound can also be used to imitate sounds like the breeze or secret conversations to add the air of mystery.

Because it still comes across so soft, it can lack energy, leading the audience to experience sadness or longing. Pianissimo doesn't always represent sadness; it can also just show emotional depth. In Chopin's "Nocturne Op. 9 No. 2," he uses *pianissimo* to create soft music with the illusion of intimacy and secrets.

PIANO (p)

Playing a little bitter louder but still softly can create a thoughtful, subdued mood. This dynamic might be used to show the temporary calmness in a piece. Although the loudest yet, this volume is still soft and can create a similar feeling to the calm after a storm, inviting the listener to follow the flow and ebb of the music. This level might also hint at tension coming.

Ludwig van Beethoven uses *piano* in "Moonlight Sonata" to set a subdued tone with a sense of calmness. The lower volume allows the audience to enjoy a reflective mood with hints at the coming tension.

MEZZO PIANO (mp)

A step up in the volume can portray pleasant feelings or a gentle mood. It doesn't express any strong emotions and often expresses contentment in music. It's a good volume for balanced moods that the pianist wants to portray.

"Lullaby," composed by Johannes Brahms, uses *mezzo piano* to introduce the feeling of tenderness and comfort. The piece is reminiscent of the lullabies sung to young children with pleasant sounds that flow together without sudden sound changes.

MEZZO FORTE (mf)

While you are still not playing loudly, you are no longer playing softly. The hint of loudness adds an energy to music and brightens up the sound. This level is great for communicating the lightness and hope of optimism or the warmth of excitement starting. Lacking the restraint of the softer dynamics, *mezzo forte* can express a sense of waking up or the start of an adventure.

"The Four Seasons: Spring," composed by Antonio Vivaldi, uses *mezzo forte* to create bright music that carries a sense of optimism and happiness, just like the season it so aptly describes. It brings to mind the thought of things coming alive after a hard winter and flowers blooming as everything warms up.

FORTE (f)

Without concern for playing softly, *forte* shows boldness and power in the music. The louder sound is confident and unapologetic, encouraging the notes to stand tall with the increase in energy. It allows the audience to experience passion or assertiveness in a piece. A composer can use *forte* to give a sense of living life to the fullest and with enthusiasm.

Pyotr Ilyich Tchaikovsky's "1812 Overture" uses *forte* to create boldness during the patriotic or exciting parts of the piece. The audience gets to become part of the victory and experience a feeling of enthusiasm and heroism.

FORTISSIMO (ff)

Getting even louder brings more emotion and intensity to the music. These notes can come across as excited or determined because the music is more overwhelming. *Fortissimo* is used to declare powerful feelings like fierceness, grandeur, fury, exhilaration, or awe. Often triumphant, it can also be overwhelming.

Ludwig van Beethoven showcases this volume with his "Symphony No. 5," a very famous piece that most people have heard at some point in their life. The demanding opening notes create an intense feeling right from the start, taking the audience on a ride of volume and energy.

FORTISSISSIMO (fff)

This indicates that you should play as loudly as you can to make sure that the music comes across as powerful and carries the audience. Because it is so loud, it creates an explosion of emotion that can range from joy to rage. There is almost always a sense of urgency when music is played loudly, carrying the audience along with the flow and creating visceral feelings.

You can hear *fortississimo* in Igor Stravinsky's "The Rite of Spring." It's a piece full of explosive music that conveys a chaotic energy. The audience experiences a wild element with almost overwhelming music, creating a primal experience.

SFORZANDO (sf)

Sometimes, the volume you play isn't the only way to express your feelings. *Sforzando* focuses on using sudden starts and stops to elicit feelings. When the music suddenly breaks into unexpected bursts of sounds, it can be very dramatic and almost jarring. In music, when there are urgent or heightened moments, suddenly loud or quiet music can help articulate that. Consider it similar to a musical exclamation point in a story demanding that the audience pay attention.

Wolfgang Amadeus Mozart uses many volume changes in his "Symphony No. 40." The dramatic changes keep the listener engaged and excited while the drama and tension build. A sense of urgency develops and makes the audience more emotionally involved in the piece.

CHANGES IN SOUND

To show a gradual increase or decrease in sound, there are arrow symbols around the dynamic symbols.

Crescendo, which is shown as < , means that you should gradually increase the volume and play louder. At the start of the *crescendo*, play softly and increase the sound as the arrow gets bigger. Crescendo can also be abbreviated as *cresc.*

Decrescendo is shown as > and means that you should slowly decrease your volume of playing when the arrow comes to a point. When you see the *decrescendo*, sometimes abbreviated as *decresc,* slowly start playing softer while decreasing the volume.

STRENGTH, COORDINATION, & RHYTHM EXERCISES

As you gain more experience and start stretching your skills, practicing strength, coordination, and rhythm will help you become a better pianist. Strength will allow you to play longer without hurting yourself. Coordination is what helps you be a consistent player who masters complex pieces. If you are a player who lacks coordination, you will have clumsy transitions and timing that's off.

Piano players can develop carpal tunnel syndrome without proper conditioning. It's easy to avoid by utilizing exercises and using proper hand placement. Without strength, you can also struggle with louder notes that require more power to avoid sounding weak.

Gifted piano players play expressive and fluid music, but it doesn't come without practice and conditioning.

STRENGTH

If you're planning to spend some time on strength-building exercises, you might benefit from warming up first. Gently stretch your fingers to warm up your finger tendons. Here are some great exercises:

Finger lifts: Place your hand on a flat surface and spread your fingers out. Starting with your pinkie, lift each one and hold it for a beat before slowly lowering the finger. Moving the fingers individually allows you to build strength in your hand muscles and isolate the tendons in each finger.

Ball squeeze: If you have a stress ball, fidget ball, or just a tennis ball, this is a good exercise for when you're sitting around. Squeeze the ball for 5 to 10 seconds, then release. Repeat for a few minutes each day.

Finger rubber bands: Using a rubber band, wrap it around your thumb and one other finger. Slowly pinch and release each finger several times before moving on to the next finger and doing the same thing.

Finger tapping: Just like you might catch yourself doing when you're bored, tap each finger, starting with your pinkie and moving to your thumb and back again.

Hand grip: You can purchase hand grippers that allow you to squeeze against resistance to improve your hand strength. Weightlifters commonly use these, and if you feel like you really need to build more strength, this is a great way to do it.

If your hands or fingers start feeling tired, take a break. You don't want to overuse your hands.

COORDINATION

Dexterity is the ability to be nimble with your hands. It comes in handy when you're playing the piano. Dexterity and coordination can help make great piano players. Here are some ways that you can improve your coordination:

Running scales: On the piano, play your scales hand over hand from one end of the piano to the other. Just doing this basic exercise will improve your dexterity.

Trill exercises: Take two fingers and place them on side-by-side keys. Play them back and forth quickly, then move to the next two fingers and repeat until you've completed every set of fingers.

Back and forth: Practice using your thumb and pinkie by placing all your fingers on keys and then playing just those two back and forth. Try to do it quickly to practice your reach.

Full 10: Place all 10 fingers on the keyboard and play each hand in sync from the pinkie inward. Being able to play multiple fingers at once is important.

Synchronized 10: Keep your 10 fingers in the same place, but instead of playing out to in with both hands, start with your left pinkie and right thumb. Play both hands across, moving at the same rate. Go faster and slower to practice different tempos.

Spider walk: Make a spider out of your fingers by arching your palm and walk across the table. Work on using your fingers in different orders to move across the surface.

Alternating rhythms: Use your right hand to start playing a slow, consistent beat from pinkie to thumb and back again. With your left hand, start playing a different beat. Concentrate and use both hands at once, keeping up the different beats. Switch the slower beat to the other hand and keep practicing.

HANON EXERCISES

For an extensive list of exercises, you can reference the Hanon exercises written in *The Virtuoso Pianist in 60 Exercises*. French composer Charles Louis-Hanon created them over 150 years ago, and they are considered the gold standard in piano exercises. There are 60 exercises that focus on improving strength, dexterity, precision, and speed.

Exercise 1: Place your right hand on the piano, playing C-D-E-F-G before going back to F and playing F-E-D-C. Add in the second hand and move them both hands together at the same time up and down the keyboard. In his book, Hanon gives helpful tips for each exercise. For this exercise, he recommends lifting each finger high so that you can make precise sounds.

Exercise 2: Add to Exercise 1 by increasing how complex it is. Instead of moving down the board key by key, you will skip a key every time and come back to it. Try playing C-E-D-F-E-G with your right hand. Once you have that down, add the left hand while doing the same thing. Having greater finger reach is an excellent skill to have as a pianist. Try to keep your movements smooth as you do this exercise.

Exercise 3: Once again increasing in difficulty, the third exercise introduces skipping intervals. Play C-D-E-F-G and skip to the next. Start with the right hand and move down the keyboard. Once you feel confident with one hand, add your second hand doing the same thing. Start in the middle of the keyboard and move outward away from each other. Mirroring your hands in reverse order makes your coordination better as they move apart.

Exercise 4: Have both your hands play the same notes at the same time. Start with C-D-E-F-G. Move across the keyboard to one side and back, keeping both hands the same distance apart. Move your hands in unison to practice keeping a steady rhythm with both hands in sync.

FINGER PLACEMENT
& POSTURE

No matter how much you practice, it won't matter if you don't hold your hands correctly. Where you place your hands depends on the piece, but for beginners, start with your thumb on middle C.

Keep your hand curved, fingers relaxed, and your thumb straight out. Don't lock or bend your knuckles. Think of sitting with both feet flat on the ground and your hands on your knees. Then, cup your hands, creating a C shape. That is the shape you want to move to the keyboard. Your thumb will straighten out so that it rests to the side and barely touches the piano key.

Your wrists should not hang down because it puts more weight on your fingers. Keep your wrists elevated to ensure your fingers can move lightly. A limp wrist destroys the graceful movements that draw beautiful sounds from the keys. Sometimes, you might play a piece that calls for more jarring sounds and, in that case, different wrist movements might be needed. Those situations will be the exception, not the rule.

No part of your body should be straining when you sit at the piano. If, for some reason, your lower body is uncomfortable, that can throw off the way your arms are able to carry your fingers to the keys. Make sure your feet touch the ground; if they don't, get a stool.

To make sure that your hand and arms are in the right configuration, look at your pinkie, wrist, and elbow. They should all be lined up. If there are any odd angles, then you need to adjust. Don't have your elbows sticking out away from your body or rubbing against it. They need to be able to move undisturbed and fall straight down naturally.

When you're adjusting your body, make sure to pay close attention to your pinkie. It can be the weakest finger and often doesn't keep its curve. Focus on strength building if you find yourself with a flat pinkie because a flat pinkie will drag the rest of your fingers down. Make each finger carry its weight and do its job correctly.

CHAPTER FOUR:
EXPLORING PIANO
STYLES & GENRES

The piano can be enjoyed in many ways. Because of the different styles of music, the piano has unlimited potential.

DIFFERENT TYPES OF PIANO PIECES

SYMPHONY

When you think of symphonies, the first thing that probably comes to mind is a full orchestra with a conductor and rows of musicians playing different instruments. However, music composition extends beyond symphonies. There are also symphonies condensed for piano.

A piano symphony lets a solo pianist perform large-scale pieces that are more complex and would traditionally be played by an orchestra. These piano symphonies allow an individual pianist to mimic the depth of sound that an orchestra might create.

SONATA

Sonatas are played by a piano and sometimes a secondary instrument. The word *sonata* comes from the Italian word meaning "to sound." It's a fitting description for this style of music. They are distinctive because of the format, with two to four movements of different styles. The first movement could be fast and lively, the second movement slower, the third movement very lively, and the fourth movement an energetic finale. Beethoven's "Piano Sonata

No. 14" is called the "Moonlight Sonata" and is a well-known example.

ÉTUDES

Études are shorter pieces that are more about showcasing skills while focusing on a select technical skill. They help a pianist improve finger dexterity and finger agility. While they can be written for any instrument, there are more piano etudes than any other instrument.

Dating back to the early 19th-century, *études* were originally just for honing skills but developed into short musical pieces. Chopin's "Études Op. 25 No. 9" is a great example of an *étude*. While no one can be 100 percent sure, many people believe it tells the story of Chopin's years in exile from Poland.

PRELUDES

A prelude is an introduction to a longer piece or a short piece of music that can stand alone. The earliest known preludes came from the church, where organ pieces were played to introduce longer hymns. There isn't any set format for preludes, so they can be created to suit the composer's needs. Chopin's "24 Preludes, Op. 28" is famous for its expressiveness and a good example of the emotion that can be incorporated into preludes.

NOCTURNES

Derived from Latin, the word *nocturnes* means "belonging to the night." *Nocturnes* are music that is inspired by night. They became very popular in the 19th century after John Field created the concept. *Nocturnes* are made for the piano and are played to represent the peace of night and all the other feelings that night can create in a way that only the piano can accomplish. Chopin also created "Nocturne Op. 9, No. 2," one of the most popular *nocturnes*.

CONCERTOS

A *concerto* is a large musical piece where the piano is the chief instrument, supported by an orchestra. It highlights the pianist's skills and the beauty of the piano. It is a chance for a pianist to showcase their skills and interact with all the music a full orchestra produces. Rachmaninoff composed "Piano Concerto No. 2 in C Minor," which is a prime example of a *concerto*.

IMPROMPTUS

As the name hints, an *impromptus* piece is made to be played spontaneously, allowing the pianist to express creativity and follow inspiration as it strikes. *Impromptus* is French for "unprepared" or "improvised." These free-form pieces don't have strict boundaries or form but follow the artists' whims. Franz Schubert's "Impromptus, D. 899" is a good example of *impromptus*.

BALLADES

A piano *ballade* tells a story using the music, tempo, and mood. These expressive pieces often have different speeds and volumes to convey what the composer wants the listener to experience. A well-known ballad is Chopin's "Ballade No. 1 in G minor, Op. 23," that tells the story of legendary heroes and epic battles.

FANTASIAS

Musical compositions that are imaginative and don't follow a particular type of structure are now as *fantasias*. One of the most famous examples is Mozart's "Fantasia in D minor, K. 397." There is also a Disney movie released in 1940 that's named *Fantasia*, which demonstrates the whimsical and creative freedom that *fantasias* allow.

SCHERZOS

Meaning "a joke" in Italian, this style of piano music is lively and playful. They normally don't stand alone but are part of a larger composition. They bring a whimsical and playful nature to music. Chopin's "Scherzo No. 2, Op. 31" is a prime example.

CLASSICAL MUSIC & THE PIANO

As the most common and fundamental form of piano, classical piano has a long, rich history with an array of styles. It's where piano music began its evolution. Composers have created pieces for hundreds of years, many of which are still played today.

With the piano, composers are able to create pieces that show a wide range of emotions and feelings. In the early 1600s, piano music began to become popular during the Baroque period (1600–1750) for this exact reason. Next, during the Classical period (1750–1820), many famous composers like Mozart and Beethoven became composers and started producing music, introducing new and exciting sounds.

From 1820 to 1900, during the Romantic period, composers focused on putting even more feeling into piano music. Famous musicians like Chopin and Liszt began composing pieces with much more emotional depth than before. This was when *nocturnes* gained notoriety.

During the 20th century, composers continued to build on their forefathers by creating more dramatic sounds and more technically difficult pieces. Most beginning piano players learn the basics by playing the music of the greats. Although many piano players can play the same piece, it won't sound the same because every piano player can put their special touch on it.

Classical piano shares stories and emotions. These pieces can range from happy to haunting. It isn't enough to just show off piano skills with classical piano playing. You must also understand how the music plays together to create a wide range of emotions.

Classic music has been around for a long time but is still relevant today because strong emotions are always important. Beethoven's "Moonlight Sonata" from 1801, Debussy's "Clair de Lune" from 1905, and Rachmaninoff's "Piano Concerto No. 2 in C Minor" from 1901 are good examples of piano played in the classical sense.

JAZZ MUSIC
& THE PIANO

Jazz music is exciting and often full of musical surprises. Originating in the early 1900s in the United States, jazz was a new sound that people fell in love with. Jazz pianists often make up music as they go because it's more about the experience of the music than sounding perfect.

Jazz music started in New Orleans, where a meld of cultures came together. People were immigrating from Africa, Europe, and the Caribbean, and this melting pot came together to create something fun and exciting.

Jazz is often played in small groups with instruments like piano, trumpets, and drums. The very early version of jazz was known as *ragtime*. "Ragging" is when a pianist adds unexpected rhythms to a song. Jazz continued to grow and expand past just the ragtime tunes. A lot of jazz music has a bouncy, upbeat feel to it.

There isn't another style that focuses on improvisation as heavily as jazz. While there's sometimes written music to follow, there's a lot of opportunity for adding your own touch when playing jazz. The written music with notes and chords is a guide that isn't meant to be played exactly. Use the notes and chords to create unique sounds.

Another type of jazz music is swing. Swing jazz music sounds like it's dancing with uneven rhythms that give it a lively sound. There are two main types of swing: sweet and hot. Sweet swing is all about slow, restrained music, while hot is fast and very edgy.

Jazz music is a lot of fun, but there are some constraints that help define jazz. Chords are used heavily and sometimes have more notes than normal in them. Scales are something you need to be really good at if you want to be a jazz pianist. Probably most important in jazz is rhythm. Jazz uses a strong beat but plays around to get the notes to sound like they're swinging.

"Take Five" by Brubeck (1959), "Round Midnight" by Thelonious Monk (1944), and "Autumn Leaves" by Bill Evans (1956) are good examples of jazz piano and the deep emotions it can create.

BLUES MUSIC
& THE PIANO

Blues music is about emotion and is one of the oldest forms of music in the United States. Originating in the late 1800s, blues evolved from work and spiritual songs that were sung by Black Americans. Because of the hard life they were forced to live after the Civil War, music played a vital role in their day-to-day lives. Many Black Americans often sang as they worked and passed songs down through the generations. This led to the birth of the blues.

Blues started appearing in the early 1900s, and by the 1920s, blues music had raced across the southern United States. It was extremely popular in places like Mississippi, Louisiana, and Texas.

These were the areas that the distinctive 12-bar blues emerged from.

Blues music follows a set of 12-bar structure that repeats, but even though the chords are repeating, they don't have to be played the same and can be changed to make the music more interesting. Blues music is simple and flexible. The scales in blues music are also special because they have a bluesy sound that comes across as both sweet and sad.

In the beginning, blues were primarily played on the harmonic, but as the genre grew, other instruments were introduced, including the piano. As more instruments were added, blues started getting recorded, which helped the genre gain popularity in other areas.

Through the '30s and the '40s, a movement called The Great Migration developed. As people from the South went north in search of better jobs and living conditions, music was not the only tradition they took with them. Once blues reached the larger cities, more aspects were introduced, like electric guitars, drums, and even horns. This new style of blues was nicknamed "urban blues." It was louder and much more powerful.

Going into the 1950s, blues had a huge impact on the developing rock and roll music of musicians like Elvis Presley. Then, during the 1960s, blues started to gain mainstream popularity through artists like the Rolling Stones and the Beatles. "The Thrill Is Gone" by B.B. King (1969), "Blues for Alice" by Charlie Parker (1951), and "Stormy Monday Blues" by T-Bone Walker (1947) are all amazing pieces of blues music that feature the piano.

ROCK MUSIC
& THE PIANO

Piano might not be the first instrument you think of when you picture a rock band, but the piano has a long and successful history in the rock music world. Piano brings a level of emotion that's hard to find elsewhere, and some of the most famous rock songs have their roots in piano music. While guitar might be considered the "king" of rock and roll instruments, the piano has also been a source of musical inspiration.

Rock began emerging in the 1950s when elements of blues, jazz, and country came together to create a new, energetic style of music. It started out as a faster form of jazz but quickly gained popularity and its own style. Rock and roll was about music that made people want to get up and dance.

Pianos were used to play fast, catchy rhythms and exciting melodies. Boogie-woogie combined blues music and rock. Boogie-woogie had happy, bouncy rhythms that repeated and were easy to learn and dance to.

Through the '50s and '60s, rock became bigger and louder. A large part of the change in rock came from the introduction of the electric keyboard. Electric pianos and organs allowed musicians to introduce an additional element to rock and play to large audiences with electrically enhanced volume.

Rock is known for its volume and extreme emotions. Rock ballads can carry an audience along with the story of the song and give the

76

artist a chance to express their feelings. The piano is used for softer, emotional parts and can introduce dramatic sounds as well. "Bohemian Rhapsody" by Queen (1975), "Let It Be" by the Beatles (1970), and "Piano Man" by Billy Joel (1973) are all rock songs that feature the piano and showcase its amazing contribution to the genre.

LATIN MUSIC
& THE PIANO

Another genre of music that is about dancing and features the piano is salsa music. This music focuses on rhythm, energy, and fun. The piano is an important part of Latin music and, especially salsa. This type of music traces its origins to the indigenous cultures of Latin America but also to Africa and Spain. Salsa especially has strong roots in Cuba and Puerto Rico.

Salsa takes Cuban music like mambo and the cha-cha-chá and mixes them. In the 1960s and 1970s, salsa was thriving in areas with large Latino populations, especially in New York. The word *salsa* is the Spanish word for "sauce" and explains the music well because it's a blend of spicy sounds.

The piano is an important part of salsa music, often playing a rhythmic pattern called a *montuno* to drive the beat. A *montuno* is a repeating rhythmic pattern that moves the music along at a steady beat. It's played with the left hand, leaving the right hand to play other melodies.

The piano also plays an important role in Latin jazz, which combines mass with Latin rhythms. The piano is played with other instruments in both styles of music like the congas, bongos, and brass. Those unique sounds come together to create the Latin music that is so distinctive.

Latin music has a special rhythm called *clave*. It's the blueprint that the whole band plays and the piano does its job of holding the beat steady and in time. The rhythm is an important part of salsa music that makes the music exciting.

Syncopation is also used in Latin music, which means playing notes that aren't part of the main beat. It adds an edge to the music and gives it a hint of the unexpected. Those distinguishing techniques are one of the reasons that people want to dance to salsa.

Some Latin songs like "Manteca" are still played today. Written in 1947 by American jazz trumpeter Dizzy Gillespie and Cuban percussionist Chano Pozo, it was one of the first songs that incorporated Afro-Cuban with jazz and was fully instrumental.

"Oye Como Va" is another song that is still popular. It was written in 1963 by Puerto Rican composer Tito Puente. The piano used the *montuno* pattern to fuel the song and became very popular in the 1970s. *Oye como va* means "listen to how it goes," and the song reflects that because it's all about enjoying the music and dancing with the rhythm.

Salsa dancing has become recognized around the world, and while it might not be as popular today as it was in its heyday, there is a lot of influence that came from those early sounds. Salsa music can still be heard in restaurants, clubs, and at festivals.

RELIGIOUS MUSIC & THE PIANO

Religious music is the music that worshippers use to celebrate and express their faith. The piano and organ are staple instruments in most types of religious music, including hymns and gospel.

Hymns are the oldest type of Christian music, dating back to the Greek and Roman period. These songs of praise have been sung for hundreds of years, and some are still sung today. Before the piano was introduced to religious music, chants were used. They were sung without any instrument accompaniment, and the peaceful chanting brought the members of the church together in worship.

In the 1600s and 1700s, a new type of church music called *hymns* began to emerge. Protestant churches, especially, began to bring music into worship services as a way to honor God. It was during this period that famous hymn composers like Charles Wesley and Isaac Watts began writing hymns that still play a prominent role in church services today. Wesley wrote "Hark! The Herald Angels Sing," a popular Christmas song, and Watts wrote "Joy to the World."

Pianos began to appear in churches to accompany the hymns, making it much easier for people to sing together. One of the older hymns is "A Mighty Fortress Is Our God," written by Martin Luther, the man who led the Protestant Reformation. Originally written in German, it is based on Psalm 46.

Probably one of the most recognized hymns is "Amazing Grace," written in 1779 by John Newton. Newton was a former British slave trader who found God and went from being part of the slave trade to a large part of the movement to abolish it. Following his appointment as pastor of a small church, he wrote a song of thanks for second chances.

Gospel music is another form of religious music used for worship. Gospel music as we know it today comes from the Black communities that used their music and voices to express their love for God. In the 1800s, Black churches created music that made people joyful, leading to hand clapping and feet tapping. Gospel music has a different feel than hymns.

As with hymns, the piano plays a vital role in gospel music. In the 1900s, gospel had gained popularity and spread across the country as a form of worship. Many of the original gospel songs came from spirituals, which are songs about hope and trust in God.

There are several gospel songs that are still popular today, like "Swing Low, Sweet Chariot," which originated before the Civil War. It was first written and recorded in the 1860s; before that, it was passed down orally. It is a song about hope that might refer to the biblical story of Elijah being taken to heaven in a chariot.

"Go Down, Moses" was printed in 1862 and has its roots in slavery. It was a song to express a desire for freedom and refers to the

Israelites who were rescued from Egypt by Moses at God's command.

Over time, gospel music has developed in many ways, but it is still a part of church worship today and brings joy like it was intended to—with the piano leading the way.

FOLK &
THE PIANO

One of the oldest styles of music, folk music, was created by people passing on their culture. Sometimes, the music was about their lives, their traditions, or their struggles. Songs often contained knowledge that people wanted to pass down to future generations.

Folk music is different in each country, region, and culture because it developed locally. Basic instruments like guitars and fiddles were the instruments that were used to develop folk music, but the piano gained an important role in that genre of music too.

Long before people could record music, music was played at gatherings or even at home. The songs featured familiar topics like farming, love, death, and legends. In America, folk music came from the early settlers who brought their own styles of music with them, blending together European ballads, African rhythms, and influences from Native Americans.

Many of the folk songs we still sing today came from those early settlers in the 1800s. Some of the famous folk songs that came from that time are "This Land Is Your Land' and "Oh! Susanna." In the early 1900s, people began recording folk music to save it for future generations.

Since folk music was often played outside at gatherings or other places where portable instruments were needed, the piano wasn't practical for folk music. But in the 20th century, when radio and recorded music became popular, folk musicians started adding in the piano along with other instruments. The new instrument added depth to the simple folk music, making it even more enchanting.

From the 1940s through the 1960s, a folk revival took place. Musicians like Pete Seeger, Woody Guthrie, and Joan Baez started making folk music popular again. They used folk music to communicate about subjects such as social justice, human rights, and anti-war themes. Bob Dylan also added more to folk music by blending other genres and the piano with it, like in his song "The Time They Are A-Changin."

Folk music has been a big part of every culture's history, and the piano was incorporated into that once the technology caught up. America isn't the only country to have folk songs; every country has its own.

In England, "Scarborough Fair" is a famous folk song. It dates back to the medieval period and was named for a town in North Yorkshire that had an annual fair. The fair brought people together from all over the country, so it was a well-known attraction. In the song, a man sends a message to a past lover, instructing her to do ridiculous tasks to get back his love. In the song, the phrase "parsley, sage, rosemary, and thyme" is used often, possibly symbolizing traits like faithfulness, courage, and love from that time.

In Japan, "Sakura Sakura" is a well-known folk song about cherry blossoms and their beauty. Cherry blossoms are a widely accepted sign of spring for Japan. The song originated in the 1600s as a children's song that taught them to play a basic instrument, the *koto*. The song is still played at festivals and other events.

The song "Danny Boy" originated in Ireland. The tune of the song was originally "Londonderry Air," but Frederic Weatherly, a lawyer, created new lyrics in 1913. It's a sad song about saying goodbye to someone that includes the lyrics "If I am dead, as dead I well may be," indicating they won't get to see each other again.

"Shosholoza" is a traditional folk song from Zimbabwe. It became popular with miners as a work song in the late 1800s. The word *shosholoza* means "to move forward."

Wherever humans gather, music inevitably thrives, resulting in diverse global folk traditions. The piano just added to an already rich history.

THE SILVER SCREEN & THE PIANO

Another place that the piano left a big impression is on the silver screen. Movies use the piano in many different ways. The movie tracks on your favorite movies help control the emotional tone of the scenes and can move the viewer to tears, joy, or any other emotion the producers want. The music in a film is called a *score*.

The first films were silent, but there would often be live music playing at theaters while the movie was going on. The piano was commonly used to accompany silent films because it could provide a wide range of sounds.

As silent films changed into talking pictures in the 1920s, music started being added directly to the films instead of relying on live music. Film composers began to write songs specifically for different scenes and movies. Because the piano has such a depth of sound and so many flexible notes, it is used in a lot of famous films. Some of the films that use the piano heavily are *Forest Gump* (1994), *The Piano* (1933), and *La La Land* (2016).

One of the first films to have live music was in 1915's *The Birth of a Nation*, but the first movie to have recorded music attached to it was 1926's *Don Juan*. Both these movies showcase pivotal times in the film industry, and the piano was right there helping play the tunes.

CHAPTER FIVE:
PERFORMANCE, CREATIVITY,
& EXPRESSION

There is nothing more satisfying than using your skills to create something wonderful and unique. Once you've mastered the skills of the piano, it's time to put those skills to work and see if you have what it takes to compose your own masterpieces.

IMPROVISING ON PIANO

Improvising means that you're creating something without preparation. Instead of reading a piece of music, you play something that comes from your heart or off the cuff of your sleeve. Improvisation isn't about creating something perfect; it's about starting something that you can build on if you want.

When you improvise, it's like having a conversation with the piano through notes, scales, and chords. Starting with the scales, try adding and taking away notes to see how they sound. If you add in different sharps, flats, and natural notes, you'll create new sounds. Experiment until you find something you like.

While it's nice to be able to sit down and play music, you truly reap the rewards of piano playing when you can sit down and express your feelings, thoughts, and hopes through the music. It also gives you confidence because you can demonstrate such an impressive skill, and you know that you will always have a creative outlet.

Besides the ability to create music and express yourself, improvisation also helps you better understand music theory and how different parts of music sound together. If you're focused on classical piano playing, you might not have as many opportunities to utilize improvisation as other genres, but it's something you still need to practice.

Spending time improvising is great for beginners, not just experienced players. That time will help you learn to relax at the piano and get comfortable with the keys, pedals, and sounds. You will quickly realize that there aren't right or wrong notes, just different sounds.

HOW TO PLAY
BY EAR

Playing by ear means that you can listen to something and then turn around and play it without having sheet music. Only a small percentage of people are naturally gifted with this ability. For most people, playing by ear is a skill that you have to practice and master.

While playing by ear isn't a requirement to play the piano, it does make you a better pianist and expands the music you can play. To start playing by ear, you need to take the time to learn the sounds of the different notes. The easiest way to do that is to have someone help you. Turn your back to the piano and have them play one note, followed by another note.

Your job is to figure out which of the notes is higher and which is lower. When you first do this exercise, the two notes should be played far away. As you improve, move them closer together, making it harder to figure out which one is which. Eventually, you might be able to start identifying individual notes just by hearing them once.

Next, choose a song that's easy with a slow tempo and simple melodies that you can get the sheet music for. Listen to small bits of the song and try to find the notes that match on the piano. Once you think you have it figured out, compare it to the sheet music and see if you figured out the right notes.

There are simple pieces that focus on improving your ability to play by ear. A lot of times, they break the songs down to the right hand first, the left hand second, and then both hands together to see if you can still pick out the notes.

You might have heard someone say they are tone deaf or been told that yourself. While amusia, or tone deafness, is a real thing, it's much rarer than you might expect. Only four percent of the population is truly tone deaf. For everyone else claiming to be tone deaf, they just haven't trained their ears to pick out the individual notes. It's a skill like any other, and it takes practice to improve it.

Even if you are truly tone deaf, you can still learn to associate notes with their sounds and pick them out to play by ear. The notes might just sound a little different to you, and you might have to rely on memory more than natural skill.

COMPOSING YOUR FIRST PIANO PIECE

When you get used to improvising, it's time to start creating your own music. Remember that music is just a matter of playing notes and adjusting them to make the sound and emotions you want. It's easy to start with a chord and build from there.

For example, let's start with the C scale (C, D, E, F, G, A, B, and C) because it's a simple, straightforward scale. You might want to build suspense in your piece by drawing out the notes. It might turn into C, C, D, D, E, E, F, F, G, G, A, A, B, B, C, and C. You've now changed the scale to fit the sounds you want to play. Now, you have a melody.

As you're playing, make sure to jot down any note combinations that you like because it might be hard to remember them once you start creating more than one. After you've played around with scales, it's time to add more dimension to your music by introducing chords.

For example, you can use your scale but replace some of the notes with the C chord (C, E, and G). You'll wind up with C, C major triad, D, D, E, C major triad, F, F, G, G, C major triad, A, B, C major triad, C, C.

Once you create several chords that you like, start trying to string them together. You might have to create transitional parts to pull all your chords together, but as you do that, music should start to develop. With these combinations of notes and chords, you now have a harmony. Keep playing around with the combinations to see what sounds you can create, and which ones match the energy you were aiming for.

Next, it's time to start using your left hand to add in depth of sound while your right hand continues to play your chords. If you listen to the sounds that both hands create together, you'll start to hear your unique music. This is where composers develop their own sounds. The amazing part of this is that you don't have to do anything special. Just sit down and enjoy playing the piano.

Keep adding to your piece by changing the tempo and dynamics or introducing articulations to the notes. While you don't need to have any idea what notes you will be playing at the start of composing, it can be helpful to have a feeling in mind. Decide whether you want an upbeat, happy sound or a dark, moody nocturn. If you know where you hope to wind up, it becomes easier to get there.

DEVELOPING YOUR OWN STYLE

As you get more familiar with creating your own music, you might find that you gravitate toward a certain genre or style. To start developing your own styles of playing, listen to composers and artists that you like to see if you can find the commonality between them. When you start paying attention, you'll probably find that your music has some of the same notes, chords, or transitions. Start with those and tinker with them to create new sounds that still appeal to you.

Before you decide that you have a set music style, take some time to listen to a diverse range of music. You might find music that you haven't been exposed to before that resonates with your preferences. Some people lean heavily into one genre like jazz or pop, while others take pieces from all music and use the parts they like. There isn't any right or wrong way to define your musical identity; it's all about finding out what makes you happy and encourages your musical journey.

The more you practice improvisation, the more you will hear the music that appeals to you. When you sit down at a piano, you will be drawn to the melodies and harmonies that you prefer. Another good method to help you develop your own style is to play chords you don't like so that you can pinpoint the sounds you'd rather avoid.

No matter how long you play piano, you won't ever stop creating your personal sound, and that distinctive sound is what will let you be a piano composer as well as a player.

USING TECHNOLOGY TO IMPROVE YOUR PLAYING

If you find that old-fashioned sheet music and sitting at the piano isn't the most effective way for you to learn, there are a lot of options where technology can help you.

Interactive apps can help you improve your piano skills, whether you're a beginner or an expert. The most common feature that these apps use is audio recognition to check your playing and listen for any mistakes. You can then get suggestions for where to improve or correct your mistakes. In order for these apps to be effective, you need to make sure you have a microphone or some other way for your device to "listen" to the music.

Along with audio, there are also video recording options that you can use. With these videos, you can work with online teachers who will look at your finger placement and technique to show you how to improve.

If you enjoy playing new sheet music and finding challenging pieces to try, you can benefit from digital sheet music libraries. Just like your local library, they offer material so that you don't have to buy each individual piece. They provide classical and modern options with several different libraries to choose from.

If you decide to try improving your ability to play by ear, there are apps and online resources for that as well. There are exercises on recognizing different notes, scales, and tones. While having a friend help you is great, it isn't always possible to get someone else to help you improve your skills.

RECORDING YOUR PIANO PLAYING

When you're first starting out, recording your piano playing can help you track your progress and listen to the improvements that you make. If you like to improvise, having a recording can also help you remember your music so that you can replicate it when you want.

After you become more proficient at playing piano, you might decide that you want to record your music and share it with other people.

HAVING THE RIGHT SETUP

To capture high-quality sound, you need to have the right equipment. A simple smartphone or tablet will do the job in the beginning, and it's something you probably already have on hand. Once you get ready to take more advanced audio recordings, you'll want to invest and upgrade your equipment.

One of the first pieces of equipment you'll need is a high-caliber microphone that can record your playing in the best possible quality. Microphones can range from under $100 up to several hundred, depending on the brand and model you choose. If you're using a digital keyboard, you won't need a microphone, but you will need a MIDI connector that will be used to record the sounds digitally.

The ATR2100x is a good microphone that's under $100. It's USB friendly and does a good job of filtering out background noise. When you get ready to look at something more studio level, microphones like the Neumann TLM 103 are able to catch detailed sounds. They typically run over $1,000.

Once you understand how you're going to record your music, you need to make sure that you have high-quality recording software. The software will save, record, and digitally enhance your music. There are free programs that work well for beginners, but if you decide you want to move into a more professional capacity, investing in a good program is a good idea.

DAW is a free program that's open source. You can attempt the basics of recording and editing your music there. Trying a free program will give you an idea of whether to invest in a more costly version. The Logic Pro is one program that has much more extensive features that are used by professionals; a program like that can run over $200.

MAKING SURE YOUR PIANO IS READY

Before you get ready to start recording, you need to make sure that your piano is in good condition. If your piano hasn't been tuned, have someone do that to confirm that everything is in the correct pitch.

Place the microphone as close to the soundboard as you can get it. The closer it is, the clearer the microphone will pick up the sound. For an upright piano, you can place it directly behind the piano and it will pick up the sound.

Wherever you decide to do the recording, make sure to have minimal sound interference. Using heavy sound-dampening curtains can block noise from your outside windows. Put a rug down or have a sound-absorbing floor so that the sound doesn't bounce and echo. If there's any kind of fan causing air movement, be sure to turn it off.

Once you get ready to make more professional recordings, it might be helpful to put up soundproofing panels or heavy blankets around the room to block out more sound. Make sure to have a "recording in progress" sign to put up if you live with other people because a door opening can ruin your audio.

When you get ready to start recording, do a short piece to see how it sounds or if any adjustments need to be made. Chances are that you won't get it right on the first attempt, so starting in smaller segments allows you to understand how your recording equipment works.

Once you have a recording that you're happy with, use your software to edit, trim, and adjust the sound. With fully edited music, you can share it with friends and family or look into sharing it on a wider scale. There are places online where you can share your music publicly and see what people think about it.

If you decide you want to consider being a more professional player, start a portfolio with all your best pieces in it. That way, you can set up a website or send your digital portfolio to music producers. You may even be able to find competitions that will accept digital or video entries. The more public feedback you receive, the more you can understand how to improve your playing.

PERFORMING AS A PIANIST

When you're preparing to take to the stage as a pianist, the most important preparation you can do is knowing your music well and being comfortable with it. A true pianist knows their pieces inside and out so that they can focus on the emotional story their music tells instead of technical aspects.

Once you're really comfortable with a piece, you can add in your own interpretation of the music and create an experience that is unique. A true sign of comprehension is memorization of your music. While having sheet music in front of you can be beneficial, it isn't required, and pieces that you have memorized come much more alive.

As a pianist, when you walk onto the stage, you should walk calmly to the piano; walking quickly or rushing makes you look nervous. Once you reach the piano, turn and bow to the audience to acknowledge the audience and any applause you receive.

Take a seat on the bench on the side farthest from the audience. Slide toward the audience to get in position. Keep your back straight and shoulders relaxed so that your arms and hands can move freely.

Before you begin playing, rest your hands in your lap and make sure that you're collected. Starting your piece with composure will help you avoid any anxiety that could taint your music. If you start while you're still trying to settle, your music can gain an anxious feeling until you find your rhythm.

If you're playing multiple pieces, make sure that you're taking a short pause between each piece. The pause allows the audience to finish feeling the music and indicates that a new piece will be starting. Don't fidget during the pause because it can draw the audience's attention away from the music.

While you're playing, keep in mind that your facial expressions and body language are also on display. While part of your face might be away from the audience, be conscious that the audience can see some of it. Keeping your body language loose and flowing allows the audience to follow the music wherever the story goes.

If you notice that the acoustics aren't portraying the sound correctly, you need to adjust the speed or level of your playing. Different venues might need different dynamics and techniques.

Once you're done playing, take a moment and rest your hands on your lap before getting up and calmly walking off stage. Save any excitement or disappointment you might feel until you are off the stage. Most audiences won't pick up when you make small mistakes so don't give it away by reacting on stage.

When you make a mistake, keep going because it will only become more apparent if you have to stop and restart. Being able to smoothly transition over mistakes is a skill that more skilled pianists have. Mistakes are almost guaranteed to happen. Keeping your facial expressions, body language, and playing steady will ensure the least amount of disruption to your piece.

PERFORMING WITH CONFIDENCE

No matter what instrument you play, it's important to play with confidence. Before any performance, you should make sure you practice, practice, practice. Confidence comes from being prepared and sure of your skills. When you're practicing, focus on the parts of your piece that are hardest. While it might be more fun to play the easier parts, that isn't where you'll get tripped up.

Your environment will also affect you. When you're familiar with a space, you'll be more comfortable playing because familiarity breeds comfort. Think about how you feel playing at your normal piano and the level of comfort you have there compared to playing in strange places on unfamiliar pianos.

Practicing at your performance venue beforehand can help you be more comfortable on the day of your performance. Take any and all opportunities to play in varied venues. The more you expose yourself to different opportunities, the more comfortable you will feel playing anywhere.

Before you go on stage, envision playing amazingly and confidently. The clearer you can picture yourself doing well and the audience loving your performance, the better you will do.

Visualization is a technique that helps build confidence and prepares you for anything in life, not just performing.

Many people suffer from performance anxiety or stage fright, making it hard to go out in front of other people to perform. If you're a performer who suffers from stage fright, that doesn't mean you can't be a great performer. There are even tricks that can help you.

Before you go on stage, allow yourself enough time to take deep breaths and practice calm, steady breathing. Slow inhales with long exhales calm your nervous system and lower your anxiety levels.

Avoid negative self-talk. Anytime you talk about your playing, your music, or your performances out loud or to yourself, make sure to keep it positive. When you do have doubts about your abilities, use positive affirmations to replace those negative feelings.

When you are on stage, it isn't about you; instead, focus on the music. If you center yourself around the music, it leaves less room for you to question yourself. If you still feel nervous before a performance, view those feelings through the lens of excitement. Could the butterflies in your stomach be excitement instead of nerves?

Another way to help yourself have confidence is to dress for success. You might have heard the term when talking about a job interview, but it can also apply to performing, even if that isn't your full-time job. When you put extra effort into how you look and how you're dressed, it gives you more confidence and makes you feel better about yourself. Another way to make sure your outside appearance matches how you feel on the inside is to smile.

Being a confident musician is about skill and attitude. Make sure you give yourself every chance to be successful.

CHAPTER SIX: FAMOUS COMPOSERS & THEIR MASTERPIECES

There have been many famous piano composers throughout the history of the piano who have left their unique influence for future generations.

JOHANN SEBASTIAN BACH

Born on March 31, 1685, Bach was a German native who became known for his many compositions. He was born into a family of musicians and exposed to music from a young age. He was the youngest child of musician Johann Ambrosius Bach and Maria Elisabeth Lämmerhirt, but his mother passed away in 1694, with his father following just months later. It is unclear how his parents passed away, but by the time he was 10 years old, Bach was an orphan.

He had an older brother, Johann Christoph, who took him in. His brother was an organist, so music continued to be a large part of Bach's life. He started learning about the works of German and Italian composers while studying the keyboard. Even as a young boy, he showed true talent for playing and creating music, and these talents are what led him to become such an influential part of Baroque music.

Baroque music was created from 1600 to 1750 and is known for its ornamentation, extreme contrasts, and deep bass line. Baroque was a new style that opened the door for future types of music like opera, *cantata*, and *sonata*.

Bach continued his musical education at a prominent musical school: St. Michael's School in Lüneburg. It was a two-week journey to get to the school, and Bach and a close friend undertook it on foot in order to attend. His time at a prestigious school allowed Bach to rub elbows with nobility from a nearby school and expand his circle of influence throughout Europe.

In 1703, after being turned down for another job, he started work as a violinist in the chapel of Duke Johann Ernst III. He was well compensated and had a piano specially tuned to allow him to create pieces within a wider range.

In 1708, he accepted a position as court chamber musician for Duke Wilhelm Ernst, the older brother of Johann Ernst. It was during this time that he composed many of his well-known works, including "Toccata and Fugue in D minor." He started gaining a reputation for his ability to blend complex melodies with beauty to create technical pieces that engaged audiences.

While he was in that position, Bach was responsible for teaching music to apprentices of the court. He was not a good teacher because he expected more than the students were able to give. Tensions grew between Bach and the students because they didn't take music as seriously as he did, and Bach had no patience for such waste.

Not only did Bach not get along well with his students, but the duke's nephew also did not understand or appreciate Bach's dedication. He often set the students and Bach at odds.

In 1717, Bach decided he needed to move somewhere that would appreciate his style of music and teaching. Whether it was because the duke didn't want him to leave or because he had fallen so far out of favor, Bach was jailed for almost a month.

While it was a trying time for Bach in Weimar, he did meet his wife, Maria Barbara, during that time. They wed in 1707 when he was 22 and she was 23. The couple shared a deep love of music and had seven children together.

Catharina Dorothea: Their first child was born in 1708 and went on to become a singer, who Bach was very proud of. She lived until 1774.

Wilhelm Friedemann: Their first boy was born in 1710 and inspired his father to put together the collection *Klavierbüchlein für Wilhelm Friedemann Bach*. While Wilhelm started in law, he turned back to music but never was able to achieve any success.

Johann Christoph and Maria Sophia: Born in 1713, Johann didn't survive, and Maria passed weeks later.

Carl Philipp Emanuel: Born in 1714, he was an inspiration to his father, who wrote lighter, more classical music after his birth.

Johann Gottfried Bernhard: Born in 1715, he went to law school but died of a fever at 24.

Leopold Augustus: Born in 1718, Leopold didn't make it to a year, passing away at 10 months old.

Bach's next job sent him to Köthen as music director for Prince Leopold of Anhalt-Köthen, an ardent music lover. The prince's support allowed him to experiment with instrumental compositions and write his most famous pieces. During that period, he wrote *Brandenburg Concertos*, *The Well-Tempered Clavier*, and four orchestral suites.

On July 7, 1720, while Bach was out of town with the prince, his wife passed away unexpectedly. By the time he made it back, she had already been buried. A year later, he met Anna Magdalena Wilcke, who was 16 years younger than him and a very talented singer. They wed on December 3, 1721.

In 1723, Bach accepted a position as a director of church music in Leipzig. His duties included directing the St. Thomas School Choir and supplying St. Thomas Church, St. Nicholas Church, New Church, and St. Peter's Church with music.

While he was in Leipzig, he composed over 300 *cantatas*, known as the *Bach Cantatas*, with only 200 surviving. He was expected to perform a *cantata* every Sunday and for all the holidays, and although he wrote mostly new ones, they were adapted from his previous works.

Bach and Ana Magdalena had 13 children during the years that Bach worked in Leipzig:

Christiana Sophia Henrietta: Born in 1723, Christiana passed away shortly after her third birthday.

Gottfried Heinrich: Born in 1724, records show that Gottfried might have had a mental disability, but he went on to become an accomplished keyboardist. He moved in with his younger sister, Elisabeth, instead of striking out on his own.

Elisabeth Juliana Frederica: Born in 1726, Elisabeth married one of her father's pupils. The couple went on to have one son whom they named Johann Sebastian, but he passed away at an early age. Her husband, John Christoph Altnikol, passed away as well, but his brother continued to provide for Elisabeth.

Ernestus Andreas: Born in 1727, he only survived two days.

Regina Johanna: Born in 1728, she passed away before she was five.

Christiana Benedicta: Born in 1730, she only lived for three days.

Christiana Dorothea: Born in 1731, she only lived to be 17 months old.

Johann Christoph Friedrich: Born in 1732, Johann Christoph went on to become a composer of some renown along with his son.

Johann August Abraham: Born in 1733, he lived for only one day.

Johann Christian: Born in 1735, Johann Christian had a successful music career, even instructing Princess Charlotte. His father was 50 when he was born.

Johanna Carolina: Born in 1737, there aren't many records of her, but she lived until 1781 and never married.

Regina Susanna: Born in 1742, she lived until 1809.

Beyond Germany, Bach was not well known or appreciated. The complexity of his music hindered its popularity at the time. Today, he is considered one of the most influential composers of all time. His music is performed and admired by audiences everywhere.

Although he didn't pass down wealth to his family, the one thing he did pass on was his love of music. His family is one of the most talented musical families in history and provided many pieces that are still played today.

In 1750, Bach lost his eyesight and underwent surgery but died from complications. Bach composed over a thousand works, dabbling in every genre of the time. All reflected his unique talents.

LUDWIG VAN BEETHOVEN

Born on December 17, 1770, to parents Johann van Beethoven and Maria Magdalena Keverich, Beethoven was exposed to music at an early age. The family lived in Bonn, Germany, at the time of Beethoven's birth. He was one of seven children, but only three survived into adulthood: Beethoven and two of his younger brothers.

From the time that Beethoven was young, he was trained in music by his father, a musician for the court and second-generation musician. With both his father and grandfather being moderately successful in music, there were high expectations for Beethoven to succeed musically.

His father, a known alcoholic, began training Beethoven when he was just four years old, forcing him to play long hours in hopes that he would become a prodigy like Mozart. One of his other instructors, Tobias Friedrich Pfeiffer, a friend of his father, would often pull him out of bed at night to practice. Despite the harsh treatment, it was obvious that Beethoven was a truly talented child, and his father hoped to be able to profit from his son's talent.

At 10 years old, Beethoven started studying with Christian Gottlob Neefe, a prominent musician who nurtured Beethoven's talents. Neefe introduced him to the works of Bach and similar artists who impacted Beethoven's love and understanding of music. It was Neefe who helped Beethoven develop his ability to compose.

By the time Beethoven was 11, he was a well-known local musician. The following year, with the help of Neefe, he published "Nine Variations on a March by Dressler." When he was 14 years old, he was named assistant court organist under Neefe at the court of the Elector of Cologne, Maximilian Franz, an experience that was rare for his age.

The small salary he earned working at court allowed Beethoven to support his family as his father's drinking spiraled out of control. Just as his father hoped, Beethoven was the family's main breadwinner by the time he was in his teens.

In 1787, Beethoven was given the opportunity to travel to Vienna but was unable to stay because of his mother's deteriorating health. His mother was his sole parental support and passed away when he was just 16 years old, leaving him as the only responsible person to care for his younger siblings. Her death was a blow to Beethoven, who often referred to her as his best friend.

When he was 21, Beethoven moved to Vienna with support from the Elector and Neefe. While there, he was able to learn under Joseph Haydn. Haydn did not teach him for long because Beethoven found it a lacking experience, but he did find other teachers to learn from such as Johann Albrechtsberger and Antonio Salieri.

His reputation quickly grew as he played at more gatherings, and within years, he was known for his passionate playing style. During this period, he composed several of his earlier works, such as "Piano Sonatas Op. 2" and "String Trios Op. 3." After a time, he was able to gain patrons who supported him and provided financial security. Count Waldstein and Prince Lichnowsky were two of his supporters.

Into the 1800s, Beethoven began to struggle with his hearing, and it quickly deteriorated. By 1802, he thought his career was over. During a low point, he retreated to the small town of Heiligenstadt, and there considered suicide, going so far as to write his brothers a letter later called the Heiligenstadt Testament.

Deciding that composing was his life's work, he resolved to continue. The following years are known as his "heroic" period, and it was during this time that he wrote some of his most iconic works. He wrote "Symphony No. 3" in 1804 and dedicated it to Napoleon Bonaparte. Beethoven admired him because of his democratic ideals and removed his dedication when Napoleon declared himself emperor. This was the first piece to truly establish Beethoven as a revolutionary composer.

Working past his deteriorating hearing, Beethoven continued to compose and perform. He learned to use special tools to feel the vibrations of his piano, and his fame continued to spread. By 1815, Beethoven was almost completely deaf. He stopped playing in public and instead worked on composing. This time is known as his late period, and since speaking had become difficult, Beethoven dedicated himself completely to music and started creating more complete pieces.

During this period, he also fought for and gained custody of his nephew, Karl. His younger brother passed away at the age of 41, leaving behind his 9-year-old son and wife. Beethoven didn't think that Karl's mother, Johanna, was a fit parent because she had previously been convicted of petty theft. Originally, shared guardianship was given to both Johanna and Beethoven, but he did not settle for that and spent years in court to gain sole custody.

Beethoven was a strict parent and had high expectations, much like his own father. The relationship was so strained that, in 1826, Karl attempted suicide, horrifying and devastating Beethoven.

Even with no hearing and personal issues, Beethoven created some of his most amazing work during those years. "Symphony No. 9" was completed in 1824, and it was his first work to have a choral movement. He was on stage beside the conductor during the premiere, facing away from the audience. Without hearing, he had no idea the reception the audience had until one of the singers on stage turned him around to see the standing ovation. Although he wasn't able to hear the applause, it was a performance that cemented his reputation.

He wrote "Late String Quartets" and "Missa Solemnis" during this time as well. Since "Missa Solemnis" was written for Archduke Rudolph's installation as archbishop, it was much more religious than his previous works.

In 1827, Beethoven's health began declining, and he passed away on March 26 at the age of 56. A funeral was held with thousands of people attending, and he left behind a legacy of moving music that is still felt today.

FRÉDÉRIC CHOPIN

Born in Żelazowa Wola, Poland, on March 1, 1810, Frédéric François Chopin was the second child and first son of Nicolas Chopin and Justyna Krzyżanowska. He had an older sister and two younger sisters.

When Chopin was six months old, his father, a native Frenchman, took a job as a French instructor at Warsaw Lyceum, a school in the Saxon Palace. The family lived on the palace grounds, which allowed Chopin to be exposed to more educated social circles. Therefore, even though they were poor, the family was extremely cultured. Creativity and intellect were praised and encouraged. Since Chopin was a sickly child, he was probably encouraged to focus on creative and intellectual pursuits.

His father played the violin and flute while his mother sang and played the piano. Although his parents exposed him to music and might have taught him the basics, his first professional tutor was Wojciech Żywny in 1816. It was obvious early that Chopin was a prodigy, and by the time he was seven, he was playing publicly and composing his own music. He published "Polonaise in G minor" and "Polonaise in B-flat major," capturing the attention of the Warsaw music community.

By eight years old, he was earning as much as Mozart, another child prodigy. In 1817, the palace was taken over for military use, and the family moved to another building. Chopin was often invited to play with the son of the Grand Duke, Konstantin Pavlovich of Russia, the ruler of Russian Poland. During those occasions, he would play for Konstantin.

He spent the next several years receiving an education at the Warsaw Lyceum, focusing on musical theory and composition. In 1824, he was on vacation visiting a schoolmate's home when he encountered Polish folk music. Folk music would become a huge influence in his work.

In 1827, Chopin's youngest sister passed away, and the family made a move to a new home across the street. That was where Chopin lived until 1830. The family ran a boarding house for young men, and it was there that Chopin meet four friends and confidantes: Jan Nepomucen Białobłocki, Jan Matuszyński, Tytus Woyciechowski, and Julian Fontana.

At the age of 20, Chopin left Warsaw, hoping to start an international career. He set out for Vienna with Woyciechowski, but within a month of the pair leaving, a Polish uprising against the Russians occurred. Woyciechowski went home to enlist, leaving Chopin on his own. In 1831, Chopin decided to go to Paris and learned en route that the uprising had been put down, leaving Chopin devastated.

When he got to Paris, a cultural mecca, he decided to make it his permanent home. He gained citizenship in 1835. Yet despite his French heritage, Chopin still considered himself Polish.

Chopin found his niche as a performer in small salons with the elite aristocrats, intellectuals, and socialites of Parisian society. This form of performing worked much better for Chopin because he did not enjoy large gatherings and crowds. It also allowed him to become embedded in the elite society of Paris.

He met many other famous musicians, including Franz Liszt, who was the opposite of Chopin in many ways. The duo often worked together and played for each other, which influenced both of their music. He also became acquainted with many other composers, poets, and even the piano manufacturer Camille Pleyel.

Chopin's popularity grew, but he continued to focus on piano music instead of following in the footsteps of most composers who worked on symphonies and operas. He composed many pieces, all meant for solo piano play, including *études*, *nocturnes*, waltzes, *ballades*, and *polonaises*.

His *études* are considered some of his best work, and he developed exercises to work on select skills. They were such masterpieces that, even though they were designed as exercises, they are musical poetry. While composing, Chopin taught music to gain a steady income since he tried to avoid public performances. Through these lessons to aspiring pianists, he was able to influence the next generation of musicians.

He struggled with poor health his entire life, and it became more of an issue in Paris. He suffered from a chronic disease, most likely tuberculosis. It was not uncommon for him to suffer from extreme coughing, fever, and fatigue, leaving him bedridden. The time he was forced to convalesce frustrated him and kept him from engagements and practice. It's believed that the introspective depth of his music during this time stems from the time he was sick.

In 1836, Chopin proposed to Maria Wodzińska, a Polish aristocrat. They were briefly engaged, but her family rejected him, probably because of his health and poor financial situation. During their engagement, he wrote some of his most emotional *nocturnes*. Once the relationship was over, he composed many melancholy pieces, including a funeral march and "Waltz in A flat major, Op. 69 No. 1."

Another woman that Chopin had a relationship with was George Sand, born Amantine Lucile Aurore Dupin, whom he met through mutual friends. She was extremely independent and unique and well known for her writings on social justice. Unlike any other woman at the time, she wore men's clothing, smoked cigars, and used a male name.

When they first met, Chopin expressed a very negative opinion of Sand, but over time, they developed a close relationship that would span a decade. Sand was extremely outgoing, and Chopin was much more reserved, but she provided a level of nurture in his life that helped him manage his health and emotional well-being. In 1847, Sand became dissatisfied with the relationship, and they parted ways, leaving Chopin devastated.

She was his last romantic relationship, and the end of the relationship contributed to Chopin's declining health. She had been his companion, caretaker, and a muse for his music. Without her, he struggled to compose or perform and started withdrawing from society.

Needing income, Chopin went on a tour of the British Isles, but the trip proved to be extremely hard on him physically. The damp environment made his symptoms worse, and his strength quickly failed. During that period, he stayed with Jane Stirilng, who seemed to have feelings for Chopin and tried to take care of him. He didn't feel the same and returned to Paris.

Once back in France, he was unable to perform publicly because his health was so poor, but he continued to teach. He composed his final pieces during this time, and they are somber, reflecting his emotional and physical health. Works like his "Mazurka in F minor, Op. 68, No. 4" showcase his melancholy and lack of enthusiasm for life but demonstrate a depth that some of his early works lacked. Chopin was probably aware that his health was in a steady decline and his life was coming to an end.

Chopin was too weak to leave his apartment during the last months of his life and relied on others to take care of him. His sister Ludwika came to care for him and provide comfort because he was in great pain. Even while struggling and in pain, Chopin was noted as still being as gentile and introspective, as he had been his entire life.

At the age of 39, he succumbed to his illness. At his request, his heart was removed and preserved in cognac until it could be sent to Warsaw and interred at the Church of the Holy Cross. His body was buried at Père Lachaise Cemetery in Paris and became a site for musicians around the world to visit.

CHAPTER SEVEN:
ICONIC PIANOS &
HISTORICAL PERFORMANCES

Along with famous composers and pianists, there are historically important pianos and places that have greatly impacted music as a whole.

FAMOUS PIANOS
IN HISTORY

Many famous composers had pianos that were unique to them.

MOZART'S FORTEPIANO

One of the most famous pianos from history was Mozart's fortepiano, which was different from the pianos you see today. His pianos were smaller and lighter. The smaller size gave it a smaller range, which allowed Mozart to have more control of the sound and enabled him to create his unique and expressive music.

The hammers of his piano were also covered in leather, which meant the sound would be different depending on how the keys were used. In earlier models, piano keys were plucked, but the hammers meant the strings were struck. There were even knee levers, which later developed into pedals.

Mozart's piano became a model for the modern piano, which was originally created by Anton Walter, a well-known piano maker in the 18th century. In 1782, after moving to Vienna, Mozart got his first piano from Walter. It gave him a chance to compose some of his best-known works that have dramatic contrasts and precise expressions.

Anton Walter was a huge influence on the fortepiano during the Classical era. He moved to Vienna by 1780, which is where his oldest surviving pianos come from. He had a reputation as being an amazing craftsman, which earned him the position of Imperial Royal Chamber Organ Builder and Instrument Maker. By 1800, Walter had over 20 craftsmen working for him. After his stepson joined, the company was named Anton Walter and Son.

One of the most important contributions to the piano that Walter made was adding the back check to prevent the hammer from hitting the strings again, which improved the piano's control. The last Walter piano was made in 1825, and Walter died a year later at the age of 74.

BEETHOVEN'S BROADWOOD PIANO

Beethoven was gifted a Broadwood grand piano by Thomas Broadwood after the two met in Vienna when Beethoven was 47 years old. Broadwood learned that the composer was struggling financially and was going deaf but still composing. Beethoven so impressed him that he gifted the composer a grand piano.

The new piano was louder than any piano Beethoven had access to, which allowed him to hear his beloved music for a little longer. Wanting to make sure that Beethoven received the best piano for his needs, Broadwood invited several famous people from the musical community to his factory to help choose the piano. They signed it before it was shipped to Beethoven.

In an effort to play as loudly as possible with his worsening hearing, Beethoven was very rough on the instrument. He even added a metal attachment above the piano, trying to make it louder. Despite the solid design of the piano, it was unplayable due to roughness by 1824. It was his favorite piano of all the pianos he was able to play in his life.

Burkat Shudi in London founded what would become the Broadwood piano company in 1728, and it remains the oldest piano manufacturer today. Shudi made harpsichords for royalty, including King George II and Frederick, Prince of Wales.

In 1761, John Broadwood, a carpenter's son, became Shudi's apprentice and later married his daughter, Barbara, joining the business. He took over in 1771, giving the company the name *Broadwood* and adding pianos to harpsichords.

That first year, he produced his first square piano. Their pianos did so well that in 1793, they stopped making harpsichords altogether. During his 1848 British tour and final performance, Chopin played another of their pianos in addition to the one given to Beethoven.

As a company, they were on the cutting edge of piano manufacturing. Broadwood pianos became known for introducing metal parts to their pianos to prevent warping and enhance the power while making them louder. Despite being repurposed to produce airplanes during WWI, the company continues to operate today with many of their famous pianos on display at the Surrey History Centre.

CHOPIN'S PLEYEL PIANO

When Chopin moved to Paris in 1831, he was introduced to Pleyel pianos, which had a much more nuanced sound than the typical piano at the time. While other pianos were robust in their sound, the Pleyel piano carried a clearer tone and handled the dynamic changes that Chopin is so well known for.

Their sound originated from the smaller hammers that made them highly responsive. In some of Chopin's music, there are whisper-like sounds that he was able to produce on the Pleyel. Camille Pleyel, the owner of the company, allowed Chopin to borrow any piano he wanted at any time, and he also gave Chopin a 10-percent commission on any pianos he sold to students.

The company was founded in 1807 by Ignace Joseph Pleyel in Paris. While publishing sheet music was the company's original function, Pleyel turned to piano manufacturing pretty quickly. Pleyel gained a reputation for having quality pianos. In 1824, Camille Pleyel, Joseph's son, took over the business. He opened the Pleyel Concert Hall in 1830, which developed into a musical mecca where many famous musicians performed.

The company Pleyel et Cie became one of the most sought-after piano manufacturers in Europe. It continued to operate into the 2000s but was unable to compete with the larger companies. In 2013, the company closed its doors for good.

The Pleyel Salle concert hall originally seated 300 people when it opened in December 1839. In the late 1920s, the hall was redesigned, and the Pleyel company redid it to accommodate 3,000 people. It was completed in 1927, and great names immediately started playing there again.

The Pleyel Salle was tragically destroyed in a fire in June 1928, making it impossible to repay a loan taken out at the Crédit Lyonnais bank. The bank took over the venue, reduced the seats to 2,400 in the remodel, and kept it until 1998. It has not been a classical music venue since 2015.

JOHN LENNON'S STEINWAY MODEL Z

There are modern pianos that have made big impacts on culture as well, and they aren't necessarily anything special. John Lennon is well known for writing "Imagine" in 1971, but what you might not know is that the piano that he wrote the globally known song on was just an upright piano that had no special features or history. It was an ordinary walnut-finished piano with no customization.

The piano became an icon after his death for being the piece that helped create timeless art. In 2000, the piano was sold to George Michael for $2.1 million. He turned around and loaned it to museums and public exhibitions because he wanted the world to have access to it.

Lennon's piano proves that magic doesn't only happen on special instruments, but on the everyday pianos you will play on. The world's next masterpiece might be created on a piano in someone's living room.

PIANOS FOUND IN ART & CULTURE

Because pianos have played such a vital role in culture and history, there are many classic artworks that depict them. These pieces give us further glimpses into the profound impact that pianos have had on society.

THE PIANO LESSON (1889)

This Impressionist piece depicts a domestic scene with two young girls around a piano. The first is seated playing the piano while the other girl stands behind her. The second girl appears to be turning the pages, possibly guiding or teaching.

It's a piece known for soft brushstrokes and warm colors, including the long red gowns both girls are wearing and their brown hair. The painter Pierre-Auguste Renoir was known for his depictions of human connection and warmth.

The overall feeling of the painting is of peace and tranquility, showing what a middle-class Parisian household might have looked like at that time. The piano wasn't just to reflect music; it also showed the household status.

Renoir was known for his art that captured everyday life, mostly in leisurely activities. The piece is now in the possession of the Joslyn Museum in Omaha.

THE PIANO LESSON (1916)

In another piece by the same name, Henri Matisse portrays a boy practicing piano. The boy seems to be his son Pierre, and the backdrop is his own home. Behind the boy is a sternly depicted woman representing a piano teacher.

The piece is painted primarily gray with geometric shapes of color in greens, reds, and oranges. Since the piece was painted during WWI, the more subdued colors seem to represent the mood at the time and the rigidity that was placed on creativity.

There is a curvy bronze statue at the bottom of the painting that contrasts with the stern lines on the rest of the piece, which further stresses the conflict between art and war. On top of the piano is a metronome, which also reflects the strictness of war time.

Matisse, born in 1860 in Le Cateau-Cambrésis, France, was a major leader in the Fauvist movement and played a significant role in 20th-century art. The Fauvism movement was known for bold colors, defined brushstrokes, simple subjects, and avoidance of three-dimensional pieces.

The painting is currently on display at the Museum of Modern Art in New York City.

THE CONCERT (1664)

The artist Johannes Vermeer, a Dutch painter, was born in 1632 and is considered one of the most influential artists of the 17th century. He lived in his birthplace of Delft, Netherlands, for his entire life and took over his father's art business in 1652.

His early work was based on religion and mythology, but as his skill and career progressed, he became known for his intimate scenes portraying everyday life. In *The Concert,* he paints three upper-class figures, two women and one man, all creating music. The first woman is playing a harpsichord, the man is playing the lute, and the last woman is singing. The painting focuses on details of the interior and the wonderful use of light.

The beloved piece of art was stolen in 1990 from the Isabella Stewart Gardner Museum in Boston and hasn't been seen since. There is a $10 million reward for any information related to the piece.

MADEMOISELLE DIDAU AT THE PIANO (1869)

Created by Edgar Degas, a well-known painter and sculptor, this piece is one of his masterpieces. Degas was born into a wealthy family in 1834 and encouraged to pursue his artistic ability from a young age.

He was best known for his paintings of ballet dancers, which captured them not only on stage but backstage, getting ready. He was mesmerized by the grace and strength they possessed.

Along with his well-known ballerina paintings, Degas captured other everyday moments with great attention to motion. *Mademoiselle Didau at the Piano* depicts a young lady seated at a piano with a genuine, focused expression on her face as she plays while looking back at the viewer.

Her posture is relaxed and elegant, with lights and shadows playing across the piano. The subject was likely a friend or acquaintance of Degas, and she is wearing all black with sheet music in the background.

The painting is currently on display at the Musée d'Orsay in Paris, France.

INTERIOR WITH WOMAN AT PIANO (1901)

The artist Vilhelm Hammershøi painted *Interior with Woman at Piano*. Born in 1864, Hammershøi took art lessons from the young age of eight. He was also enrolled at the Copenhagen Art Academy from the age of 15 to 20.

To offset the rigid teaching of the academy, he took lessons at the free studio Kunstnernes Frie Studieskoler, where more unconventional styles were taught. Hammershøi became known for his work that was outside the norm at the time.

A lot of his work focused on interior scenes and subjects from behind, especially his wife, Ida Illsted. She was a common subject in all his works. In *Interior with Woman at Piano*, the scene depicts a woman sitting at a piano with her back to the viewer. Between the women, the view is a white tablecloth table with white dishes and butter on it. The clean lines, muted colors, and lack of furnishings helps establish a sense of calm and silence.

The piece is currently held in a private collection and unavailable for public viewing. In 2017, the piece sold for $9,124,350 at

Sotheby's New York, a record-breaking amount for a Hammershøi work.

MUSIC ROOM (1880)

Gustave Caillebotte, born in 1848, was a well-known part of the Impressionist movement. He was born into a wealthy Parisian family and started out as a lawyer and engineer before he discovered his passion for art.

He focused on realistic recreations of everyday scenes with an eye for detail. In *Music Room*, he stresses the important role that pianos played in the social and cultural influences of society at the time. It reflects the bourgeois society with a stress on leisure and refinement.

While Caillebotte's works are highly respected and well known, the location of *Music Room* is not well documented, and the exact value is not available. Another of his pieces, *Young Man at His Window*, sold for $53,030,000 at Christie's in New York in 2021.

ROOM IN NEW YORK (1939)

Born in 1882, Edward Hopper was a prominent American painter who specialized in realism. He focused on American life and the idea of solitude and introspection. Like most great painters, he paid special attention to light and shadows.

Hopper was born into a middle-class family in Nyack, New York. His family encouraged and supported his artistic abilities, and with that support, he went on to complete studies at the

Correspondence School of Illustrating, followed by the New York School of Art.

At the start of his career, he focused on illustrations for commercial work. He was so successful that he decided to try his hand at painting. Most of his work uses color saturation to create the mood and setting of his pieces.

Room in New York shows a man and a woman in an apartment. The man is sitting in an easy chair reading a newspaper while the woman sits across from him at a piano. It shows two people in the same room with no connection or emotional ties despite their close physical proximity.

The piece is on display at the Sheldon Museum of Art in Lincoln, Nebraska. While there isn't an exact dollar amount connected to the piece, Hopper's work is usually held in high esteem. One of his most famous pieces, *Chop Suey*, set the record for his pieces in 2018 when it sold for $91.9 million at Christie's.

MADAME MANET AT THE PIANO (1868)

Édouard Manet, born in 1832, was a French painter who helped art transition from Realism to Impressionism. He was extremely well known for his accurate depictions of modern life.

In *Madame Manet at the Piano*, he painted his wife sitting at a piano. The piece reflects real life because his wife was a pianist who met Manet when his father hired her to teach him. The piece highlights and recognizes his wife's great musical talent while portraying the domestic importance of music in their lives.

In the painting, the viewer is facing the side of Madame Manet and her piano. Her fingers are poised gracefully over the keys, and she has a focused but peaceful expression on her face. The colors are warm, and she is wearing a black dress.

Madame Manet at the Piano is in the Musée d'Orsay in Paris. While that painting is not for sale because a museum holds it, Manet's other painting, *Le Printemps,* sold for $65.1 million in 2014 at Christie's.

LITERATURE

Pianos have inspired literature as well as paintings. One of the more well-known examples is *Anna Karenina* by Leo Tolstoy. In the book, one of the main characters, Kitty Shcherbatsky, uses the piano to express herself and as an emotional release.

In the book, piano is not only a form of self-expression in Russian high society at the time but also a cultural expectation. The piano is used to represent themes of emotional complexity, societal expectations, and personal transformation.

MOVIES

Shine, the 1996 movie, is based on the life of pianist David Helfgott. It's a biographical drama that shows his life as a prodigy and his struggles with mental illness.

Amadeus, the 1984 film, is centered around the life of Wolfgang Amadeus Mozart and his musical genius. The child prodigy is shown using the piano and other keyboard instruments. The film was so well received that it won eight Academy Awards, including Best Picture.

La La Land, the 2016 movie, is about artists who go to Los Angeles to chase their dreams. One of the lead characters uses the piano as his instrument of choice.

There are many more examples of piano movies, such as *Grand Piano* (2013) and *Green Book* (2018). Pianos have played a central role in the arts, no matter the media.

LEGENDARY PERFORMANCES ON PIANO

While all piano performances can be moving and inspiring, there are some that stand out and leave the audience speechless.

FRANZ LISZT

Every one of Liszt's performances left the audience awed because of the technical skill he perfected and the emotional depth of his pieces. He was the performer who popularized the solo piano recital, and he often played from memory, something that wasn't common at the time.

One of his most legendary performances was in Rome in 1839. While he had captivated audiences across Europe, he outdid himself with that performance. Liszt performed in front of Pope Gregory XVI. He played religious compositions that elevated his abilities to new levels. The audience was amazed.

SERGEI RACHMANINOFF

Rachmaninoff delivered some of the most legendary performances of his time. The talent he was most known for was his ability to span vast chords because of his large hands. He was unmatched in his ability to give emotional depth to his music.

In 1930, he performed at Carnegie Hall, playing his "Third Concerto," which showcased all his skill. The audience and critics hailed the performance as one of the best they had seen. It was also the performance that solidified his place in piano history.

VLADIMIR HOROWITZ

During his career, Horowitz walked away from performing for 12 years, a very unusual move for someone with his talents. He needed time to handle mental health issues he was struggling with that came from constant touring and performing. The stress was too much for him and was constantly compounded by his need for perfection.

After 12 years of focusing on his health and his family, Horowitz was ready to play again, and he chose to make his comeback at Carnegie Hall. In 1965, Horowitz made his return to a sold-out house. The concert was recorded and broadcast for the entire world to hear.

Horowitz carefully curated the program with the following pieces:

- Domenico Scarlatti's "Sonatas"
- Robert Schumann's "Kreisleriana"
- Alexander Scriabin's "Étude in D-sharp minor, Op. 8, No. 12"
- Frédéric Chopin's "Ballade No. 1 in G minor, Op. 23"
- Sergei Rachmaninoff's "Prelude in G minor, Op. 23, No. 5"
- Franz Liszt's "Hungarian Rhapsody No. 2"

GLENN GOULD

While Johann Sebastian Bach music is incredible as written, Gould took it to the next level. In 1955, he recorded an album called *Bach: The Goldberg Variations,* and it became one of the most recognized performances in music history. He used precise timing, unconventional phrasing, and humming while he played.

Early in his career Gould devoted himself to studio recording because he liked the controlled environment better. He also immensely disliked playing in concert halls.

Due to his hesitation with live performances, it wasn't until 1957 that he played his interpretation of Bach's "Goldberg Variations" live on his Soviet tour. It was one of the few times he played in public. The performance left the audience astounded, and they gave him a five-minute standing ovation.

ART TATUM

A renowned jazz pianist, Tatum brought a new level of technical ability and innovation to the jazz genre. Unlike his contemporaries, he used improvisation and harmonies to stand out, and he performed pieces that defied belief.

"Tiger Rag," a traditional jazz piece by the Original Dixieland Jazz Band, was thought to be impossible to recreate, much less on the piano. Tatum completely reimagined the pieces, incorporating the famously fast song into a piano piece with cascading arpeggios, fast chord changes, and unmatched clarity. He made the first recording of it in 1933 and went on to play it live, leaving audiences stunned each time.

FAMOUS CONCERT HALLS

Not only are painters and pianists important, but there are also places where the piano is played that have made an impact on the art form.

CARNEGIE HALL (NEW YORK, UNITED STATES)

Built on May 5, 1891, Carnegie Hall is located in Midtown Manhattan. It's one of the most iconic venues in the world. Andrew Carnegie, a steel tycoon and philanthropist whose wife sang with the Oratorio Society of New York, built it. He believed she and other performers deserved a dedicated space to showcase their talents.

It cost a whopping $1.1 million to complete the building, which would be over $34 million in today's currency. The exterior is reddish-brown Roman brick, and the interior boasts thick concrete walls, making its acoustics unparalleled.

One unique aspect of Carnegie Hall has always been its policy of inclusivity. The hall was open to a wide range of artists, no matter their background, and gave them a chance to perform when they might not have otherwise had one. Many famous pianists made their debut there, including Vladimir Horowitz, Arthur Rubinstein, and Sergei Rachmaninoff.

Not only did pianists make their debut there, but they also chose to end their performing careers at Carnegie Hall. In 1986, at 82, Horowitz played his final performance there. Rachmaninoff played one of his last concerts at Carnegie Hall as well. He passed away just three months later, ending the Romantic piano tradition as it was known.

Carnegie Hall remains a performance venue for all music. It also hosts educational programs for people of all ages and conducts community outreach.

VIENNA MUSIVEREIN (VIENNA, AUSTRIA)

In 1857, Emperor Franz Joseph I decided to expand the city of Vienna by taking down the old city walls. Using the opportunity, the Society of Friends of Music in Vienna established a new concert hall with a piece of land granted to them by the emperor.

In 1863, plans for the new building started with Danish architect Theophil Hansen leading the project. He planned a Neoclassical-style building, and the project was completed in 1870.

There are several halls within the Musikverein, including the most famous, Großer Musikvereinssaal (meaning "Great Hall"). The hall measures 160 feet long by 62 feet wide and has a ceiling height of 59 feet. It was built to hold 1,744 seats and provide standing room for 300 people. The size and rectangular shape of the room help with the acoustics, a main reason that the hall is so famous.

The hall was built to help and develop amateur piano players, but it was also associated with famous pianists like Beethoven, Schubert, and Mendelssohn. Today, the building is still used for classical music and serves as the host of the Vienna Philharmonic Orchestra. The unique venue continues to be a destination for pianists and music lovers from around the world.

ROYAL ALBERT HALL (LONDON, ENGLAND)

Opened on March 29, 1871, the hall was built by Queen Victoria after her consort, Prince Albert, passed away in 1861. He dreamed of a hall to promote the arts and sciences, and while he did not live to see it, his dream has benefitted generations of artists since.

Inspired by ancient amphitheaters with an elliptical shape and dome roof, it was built with over 6 million red bricks and 80,000 blocks of terra cotta. Encircling the outside of the building is an 800-foot-long mosaic frieze called *The Triumph of Arts and Sciences*.

The hall has been the site of many events, from speeches by Winston Churchill to boxing matches to the classical music concerts held there every summer. Many famous pianists have played there, including Pyotr Ilyich Tchaikovsky, Edward Elgar, Benjamin Britten, Sergei Rachmaninoff, Claude Debussy, and Igor Stravinsky.

BERLIN PHILHARMONIE (BERLIN, GERMANY)

The original Philharmonie, which was built in 1882, housed the Berlin Philharmonic Orchestra and was a hub for classical music. Unfortunately, the building was destroyed during World War II.

Once it was decided that a new Philharmonie was needed, a competition was held to determine the architect who would lead the project. Hans Scharoun won the competition, and construction began in 1960. The official inauguration took place on October 15, 1963. The new building represented the city's commitment to the arts.

Scharoun truly outdid himself with a groundbreaking design. The building was designed as an asymmetrical structure with a tent-like draping and a stage in the middle.

Despite a devastating fire that destroyed a quarter of the roof and led to severe water damage in 2008, the building continues to be used today. It hosts an array of cultural events for music and the performing arts.

PALACE OF VERSAILLES (VERSAILLES, FRANCE)

A symbol of French history and devotion to the arts, the Palace of Versailles was built into the showcase it is by Louis XIV. Originally, the building started out as a hunting lodge for Louis XII, but in 1682, Louis XIV moved the capital of France to Versailles. With this move, he redesigned the palace to be a symbol of the power and grandeur of the French crown.

Construction began in 1661, with the work being led by architects Louis Le Vau and, later, Jules Hardouin-Mansart. It wasn't until 1682 that the palace was inaugurated, and the royal court moved in. The expansion of Versailles was never ending, growing over the next several decades to the point that it strained the royal treasury.

All the hard work and fortunes put into it made it a masterpiece and a showcase to both art and architecture. There are several key areas in the Palace of Versailles that are iconic. The Hall of Mirrors (*Galerie des Glaces*) is named for the 357 mirrors that reflect the outdoor gardens through large arched windows. It also has a Royal Chapel with an impressive organ.

The most important part of Versailles for music is the Royal Opera House. Construction began in 1763 and didn't finish until 1770. The inauguration was in celebration of the marriage of the Dauphin, the future Louis XVI, to Marie Antoinette. It has an elliptical auditorium to enhance the music and opulent designs with gilded woodwork to amaze and entrance audiences. The ceiling is painted to depict Apollo and the Muses.

Today, the Royal Opera House is still a vibrant cultural venue, hosting performances, operas, concerts, ballets, and other events to honor the arts. It still brings people from all over the world to admire its 18th-century French grandeur.

PHILHARMONIE DE PARIS (PARIS, FRANCE)

A more recent addition to the world of piano venues is the Philharmonie de Paris, which emerged in the early 2000s. The goal of the project was to provide a state-of-the-art venue for music and, specifically, symphonic music.

In 2007, a competition was held to decide who would design the building, and architect Jean Nouvel won. Construction didn't start until 2010, and the building was inaugurated on January 14, 2015. While the budget was originally €120 million, due to overruns and delays, the final cost wound up being €381 million.

The outside of the building is covered with 340,000 aluminum panels in different shades of gray, creating a mosaic of birds in flight. The *pièce de résistance* of the Philharmonie de Paris is the Grande Salle, a 2,400-seat concert hall designed in a vineyard style with a central stage surrounded by seating for the audience.

The venue hosts musical performances from classical to contemporary and everything in between, making it an inclusive space for all. There are workshops and music education activities to engage audiences of all ages. It's a modern nod to the history of classical music.

CONCLUSION

As history has proven, pianos are more than just an instrument; they are a gateway to creativity, expression, and sharing. No matter how you choose to play, whether through improvisation, by ear, or by composing, you'll be following in the footsteps of all the great musicians who came before you. You'll move beyond technical skill as your personal connection to music grows, and you find your own voice.

Your journey with the piano should not be about perfection or to please others. Instead, it should focus on your own growth and the joy of discovering your abilities. Once you start to develop your own style, it will reflect your individuality. Whether you choose classical melodies, jazzy improvisations, or modern pop chords, you'll put your own touch on any music you play.

Utilize the technology that is available to you while you are learning and when you create. The advancements that have been made will enhance your musical experience and take your artistry to a new level. Share your music with others to showcase your skill through online platforms when you're ready.

Find what you love most about the piano and focus on that area. Whether you enjoy the technical skill, the improvisation, or the performance part, it doesn't matter as long as the piano is still a part of your creative journey.